Do Wild Baking

Food, fire and good times

Tom Herbert

Published by
The Do Book Company 2017
Works in Progress Publishing Ltd
thedobook.co

Text © Tom Herbert 2017
Photography © Jody Daunton 2017
Photography p99, 145 © Tom Herbert
Illustrations © Hannah Cousins 2017

A CIP catalogue record for this book
is available from the British Library

ISBN 978-1-907974-35-9

10 9 8 7 6 5 4

To find out more about our company,
books and authors, please visit
thedobook.co or follow us **@dobookco**

5% of our proceeds from the
sale of this book is given to
The Do Lectures to help it achieve
its aim of making positive change
thedolectures.com

Cover designed by James Victore
Book designed and set by Ratiotype

Printed and bound by OZGraf Print
on Munken, an FSC® certified paper

MIX
Paper from
responsible sources
FSC® C163799

Disclaimer
The information in this book has been
compiled by way of general guidance
in relation to the specific subject
addressed, but is not a substitute
and not to be relied on for medical,
healthcare or other professional advice
on specific circumstances and in
specific locations. Every precaution
must be taken when cooking outdoors
on an open fire and to ensure it is out
before you leave. Always tell someone
where and when you are heading
out and what your plans are. Learn
how to read a map and take it with
you. There are vast swathes of the
countryside where you just won't be
able to get a phone signal. The author
and publishers disclaim, as far as the
laws allow, any liability arising directly
or indirectly from the use, or misuse, of
the information contained in this book.

Contents

> Staying in the house breeds
> a sort of insanity, always.
>
> —
>
> Henry David Thoreau

I notice first a wisp of smoke rising above the horizon. As I approach, I hear the sound of laughter and, closer still, the crack and pop of a wood fire. It's the smell though, a warm smokiness mingled with something savoury bubbling in a pot, that draws me in.

Kneeling down, I poke the fire with a stick and stir the pot. It's satisfying and I breathe out. I catch the eye of the others and we begin to talk more freely; it feels good to be known.

A taste of the wild, an ancient thing, a good thing indeed. We know what it is to be truly alive.

Introduction

For me, wild baking represents freedom. Not in a melodramatic, chest-beating way, but as a break from the routine, a chance to re-engage and connect with nature, food and people.

Funnily enough I don't see myself as a 'chef' when I'm cooking outside, more of a fire starter. Fire and food are catalysts for, well, some good times! And in this book, to help get people in the mood, I've even suggested a few ways to spark a conversation (with a bit of input from friends on social media – thank you!).

Over the years and as my own family has grown, the campfire has become a safe space. Not just somewhere to catch up, laugh and share, but a place to have conversations that, sitting around a table, might not otherwise happen. Looking into the burning embers of a fire, rather than each other, has allowed this and I'm sure we've remained close as a family as a result.

So if this is such a life-affirming subject, why the small book? Well, I wanted to publish a cookery book – crammed with recipes and the best advice gleaned from my baking ancestors going back over five generations – yet in a portable form. Something that you can easily slip in your back pocket or bag and take with you. Plus the less time reading means more time spent outside and really living.

So I haven't filled this book with endless tips, information and novelty recipes. Just those that I know are good enough to make a micro-adventure in the wilds more delicious and successful.

When you're really away from it all and the work has been done – the food has been cooked and a bottle opened – you get the deep satisfaction that comes with sharing good food and good conversation around an open fire with people that you love. Even if you don't rate yourself as a cook, what the world's top gourmets and chefs know is that nothing in the world compares to food cooked over a fire.

One of the things that I love about baking is that every time we do it we have the opportunity to perfect what we did before. We are always prototyping and striving for perfection – and then eating the evidence. It's an art and a science and I hope to share with you a bit of both.

Urban 'wild' baking

Wild baking is more than being outdoors and it's more than baking. It's a way of cooking that is somehow more timeless, convivial, nutritious and hugely satisfying. Sometimes we need a taste of the wild but can't escape to the outdoors. Sometimes our very being yearns for the silence, the open spaces and the change of air that the great outdoors gives us for free. But, we can't get there. So what can we do? We can look at our calendar and make a commitment to a time in the near future, and meanwhile, we can eat in a wild way closer to home as a covenant to our next adventure.

Wild baking is to make your own way. Sure, some inspiration and motivation or a new piece of kit can all get us out the door. And if we are prepared, we can take our time, discover new things: the unexpected, good and bad, all make a good story. We'll share it *if* we survive! And this striking out into the wild, whether cooking or bodily, gets deep into the very fibre of who we are. It builds resilience and peacefulness, and this is something we can easily tap into in an urban setting – even if that setting is a park, or a terrace or just leaning out of a window. We can all hold a bowl of steaming, chucked together noodles and howl at the moon.

Now let's go and light a fire.

The
Essentials

Health and safety

Warning! This book carries a risk of:

— **Fire**
— **Burns**
— **Cuts**
— **Stabs**
— **Bleeding**
— **Death by starvation/dehydration/animal attack**
— **Falling**
— **Drowning**
— **Boring people to death**
— **Loss of friends**
— **Change of personality type**
— **Change of body shape**
— **Growth of character traits**
— **Poisoning** – on a serious note, when I say you can add foraged foods to a recipe (seeds, nuts, fungi), it goes without saying these must be edible. If in doubt, take a photo on your phone and cross-reference with one of the many foraging apps now available. And a few days out with a professional forager is a must: *foragers-association.org.uk*

Put simply, going into the wild, lighting fires and cooking with poorly temperature-controlled food, where light levels and visibility may be low, is hazardous. **If you are baking in the wild you do so at your own peril!**

Hygiene

You must take particular care when handling raw meat and high-risk foods such as raw fish and eggs. You might like to consider brushing up on some food safety essentials online before you venture out. Check out the one at *highspeedtraining.co.uk*

As a general rule, keep your hands clean, especially after handling raw food. A hand sanitiser gel is good and wet wipes are ideal as they can be burned afterwards. Alternatively heat some water in a pan and use the hot water (take care not to scald yourself) and soap to clean your hands. Obviously all your kit needs to be kept clean too. Always wash everything thoroughly after use and leave to dry.

How to clean a pan
Once you've emptied it as best you can, add a little water to it and some soap (I have a sample bottle of washing-up liquid for camping) and put back on the fire to heat up. It'll now be much easier to clean. Dry it by hanging from a stick near the fire.

Measurements

Assuming you're not taking scales with you, throughout the book I've used American-style cups, handfuls and pinches as far as is possible. Occasionally measurements in grams are given where absolutely necessary, or as a rough guide. And, of course, you may want to cook any of these recipes at home with the luxury of measuring jugs, spoons, scales and a roof. Recipes that are suitable for home cooking are indicated by the little house icon above.

Wild baking kit

Large heavy pan with a tight-fitting lid The weight can be a downside if you've far to go, yet it's the weight that makes it so good over a campfire. It's much easier to cook something well without burning it. A Dutch oven is perfect, and one with a hoop carry handle makes carrying it easier; you can also suspend it over a fire using a tripod, giving you more control.

Grill A trusty metal grill (the stronger the better) that you can strap to your pack and take anywhere to use over a camp fire will bring you many of the benefits of a BBQ. With a large upturned pan on top, it's possible to create a lid-on BBQ or baking oven. Go for a stainless steel model (easier cleaning) with bars not too far apart (don't lose a sausage).

Long metal tongs A long and strong pair of tongs will make cooking much easier and less 'burny' for you.

Large light mixing bowl For mixing ingredients, doughs and salads as well as washing up.

Shower cap Don't let your dough dry out! The elastic sides hold it onto the bowl, and they're reusable.

Dough scraper Super-useful for any number of chopping and cleaning tasks – see page 150 to make your own.

Measuring cup See page 45 for more.

Tablespoon/teaspoon For measuring, stirring and eating.

Chopping board Okay, so we don't want to take the kitchen sink, but do consider a chopping board. There'll be numerous times when you need something to work, chop, knead or roll out on. A thin piece of plywood is ideal.

Roasting tray Sturdy disposable foil ones are very useful.

Thermometer If you want to know your food is safe without boiling/burning all the loveliness out of it, a thermometer can give you peace of mind.

Thick oven gloves Burns aren't nice.

Wooden spoon The longer the better.

Wonderbag Okay, so it's a big bag, but it's so, so much more than that. It's basically a non-electric slow cooker, building on the tradition of hay box cooking. It also keeps things hot for up to 12 hours and cold for ages. Bonus: every Wonderbag bought buys one for a family that need one. Also makes a superb pillow.

Kitchen foil The stronger the better, so look for catering-quality stuff that won't perish in the fire.

General kit

Tarp with brass eyelets Super-useful for sleeping under, as a roof when you eat, and keeping kit dry.

Paracord For rigging stuff up, like the tarp or a stick tripod for cooking under (see page 28).

Bivi bag I only recently came across these on a micro adventure with outdoor man Al Humphreys. I immediately ordered two. Sleeping under the stars with my kids in the garden is simply a wonderful thing to do, and great training for many adventures to come. The beauty of them is that if the weather is good, then sleeping out is a doddle, and good use can always be made of the space and time you save by not packing and putting up a tent.

Small axe For making stuff or fending off beasts in the night.

Sharp knife A penknife or sheath knife is so much more useful in the wild. Learn how to sharpen it – you'll be so glad you did.

Torch Got one on your phone? Then make sure you pack a charging battery. Make a tripod from a stick with three prongs on the top, stake it into the ground and aim your phone torch at the cooking action.

Water Either take plenty – including enough to safely put out a fire – or have a water bladder and tablets to purify your water.

Drinking vessel My personal preference is to drink wine or beer from either a tough glass or an enamel or wooden cup, because the sound of the 'cheers' ting is music to my meal. And the way it feels in the hand is all part of the experience. Although the good thing about paper cups is that you can burn them at the end of the night – no washing-up! If you have a hip flask do take it with something warming in – rum or whisky are ideal.

First aid kit Don't regret not taking one. For burns, clean cold water is best.

Whistle If you get stuck, separated or lost you might need to attract attention.

Improvise!

In the wild, it's essential to see the duality of use in everything, and once you start you'll see wild baking uses for everything, often borne out of simple necessity. A wine bottle or can of beer can become a rolling pin, while a tent peg mallet can be used to bash spices.

My hero ingredients

Think of this list as your portable store cupboard.

Freshly milled organic flour So many of the recipes in this book, especially in the Bread chapter, require flour. Freshly milling my flour at home has been game changing. WTFunk? you may be thinking, but it's not very long ago that grinding your own coffee beans was unheard of, and now we all know it makes a better-tasting coffee. With flour, our decisions over which to use should be about nutrition as well as taste. And yet almost all commercial wheat is milled in such a way as to remove most of the natural goodness of the grains in favour of long shelf life.

When you mill your own flour, however, you can be sure that nothing is added or taken out. And look, it tastes so much better. In fact – coeliacs aside – I'm convinced that it's not gluten that is the cause of the discomfort that has given rise to mass gluten-freeism in recent years, but rather over-processed, mass-produced flour and bread.

The next best thing to home-milled flour is commercially stoneground. If you really don't want to get a mill and try your hand at opening the great nutritional gift of nature that grains are, then it's certainly worth sourcing a good organic flour to make sure that it contains the delicious goodness of the wheat germ. Take some time to look into it – it's your call.

Best quality strong Parmesan Flake over a savoury dish for an umami flavour boost.

Butter See page 79 for a simple recipe for homemade butter.

Cooked chorizo This spicy sausage brings great flavour and can survive better than raw meat in the wild. The fat released will grease your pan up something lovely.

Coffee Can't live without it. Great in a chilli (see page 110) and absolutely necessary in the morning (see page 141).

Dark chocolate Melt it for hot chocolate or a hot chocolate sauce or add a few pieces to give depth to a chilli. Sometimes a cube will do as pudding after a long day outside.

Dried pasta, noodles and rice Low in weight, high in carbs. Just add water and heat.

Hot sauce Bring the heat.

Lemons Complete with their own delicious and zesty skin. If a dish tastes boring, it's worth asking: would a squeeze of lemon liven it up? Plus drinking a cup of hot water with a slice of lemon makes a refreshing morning cleanse.

Marshmallows They may be a campfire cliché, they may burn your mouth and picking them out of your beard (sorry ladies) isn't a great look, but they rarely disappoint.

Oil Olive is classic but Rapeseed is produced in the UK and has a higher smoke point. My new favourite is Ghee – healthy, tasty and on point.

Scotch bonnet chillies Consider the superb ratio of weight to flavour when heading out to bake. Add them whole to a stew, casserole, chilli or curry; once the dish has enough heat whip the little chilli grenade out.

Seasoning Take a small tin of sea salt and a little pepper mill to ensure all your wild baking sparkles.

Wine and beer For drinking with friends, obviously, but also used in many of the recipes. Opt for natural and craft when going wild.

Wild Foods See page 147 for a list of the best seasonal foraged foods to add to your meals.

For the recipes, I've only included the ingredients that I think are essential to the quality of the dish. In the wild, as at home, if you wish to cook simply and create something delicious, the same care needs to go into sourcing those ingredients. No amount of skill on your part will hide the dry, tense taste of fear in meat or mask the wet worry in battery eggs. Make the ingredients you select shine. Please. Your guests will thank you.

Decide what you're going to cook

If you want to enjoy wild baking, planning is going to be important. You want to plan enough to ensure you have the right ingredients and equipment to successfully feed yourself and others, while allowing for some spontaneity to make the most of things you find along the way. Bottom line is: read the recipes right through before heading out so you take everything you need with you – and leave nothing behind when you're done.

Preparation is everything. Make sure you have everything to hand and ready for cooking before you start.

But first, let's get your oven sorted.

Fire is such a fragile and beautiful thing

—

Chef Francis Mallmann

A campfire truly is a wonderful thing: bringing light in the darkness, giving warmth on cold nights and providing energy, which we can use to cook food. Staring into a fire can provide an evening's entertainment (Netflix who?) as you notice how different woods create different-coloured flames while emitting a variety of wonderful aromas. The hiss and crackle of a fire, the throwing of sparks, the waft of smoke and the shadows dancing in the darkness create an ancient playground for the telling of stories and a home for great conversation.

A sensory experience

Baking wild requires you to use all of your senses including common sense, and of course to use and develop your intuition. We can usually smell burning before we see it but it's important to understand the difference between a charred cherry tomato (wonderful) and a charred cake (not so good). It's up to you to work it out – it's your cake, after all.

I was taught to bake on falling heat by my dad. This is when you start with the things that need the most heat and finish with those things that simmer well in the embers. It's the best way to get maximum use from your campfire.

Find a good spot

When choosing a spot, you need to consider the following:

Legal Before you even think about building a fire you need to check that you're not in violation of any local by-law. If you're on private land, make sure the owner is happy about you being there and having a fire.

Practical Okay, so you're not breaking any laws or upsetting any farmers; now you need to use your common sense and outdoor skills to select the ideal spot. Build your fire so that it is sheltered, taking into account the lie of the land and the prevailing wind.

Safe This is your fire so don't make it someone else's problem. Create a physical firebreak of open space, cleared of combustible materials. Remove any tripping hazards that could land you in the hot stuff once it gets dark. Keep flammable things covered and well away from the fire and notice the direction of wind. You don't want smoke and sparks blowing into your tent. Have a large supply of water to hand so you can put the fire out should that become necessary. Make sure the surfaces you are working on and things you are sitting on are stable and not likely to fall into the fire.

A cautionary tale

The wind once blew my stove over when my back was turned and set a cliff on fire. This was a terrifying few minutes. Fortunately I was near the sea and the tide was in so I was able to put it out, with a bag-for-life full of seawater, but while it wild-fired up and away from me, towards the homes and village above, I genuinely thought I might wind up being history's second most infamous baker after that one in Pudding Lane in 1666. I share this with you as part of my ongoing therapy. Thank you. Moral of the story: you play with fire, you're going to get burned, or worse, burn someone or something else. Put simply, have fun but please be careful.

Leave no trace

As with anything wild, the community you are part of as you venture out to bake, sleep and make merry, is encouraging, supportive and engaged. It's also TOTALLY RELYING ON YOU NOT TO SCREW IT UP AND SPOIL IT FOR EVERYONE ELSE. Leaving no trace is the most simple and fundamental tenet of wild baking. A beautiful spot will be special to other people too – it might even be sacred. If you leave scorched earth and other cooking detritus, we all get a bad reputation. The solution is easy enough. A good spot for your fire is one where you can move undergrowth to one side, even cut turf out and place to one side, well out the way, so it doesn't burn. When you have finished with your fire, douse it well with water and cautiously feel the entire area with your hands to check that there isn't anything even slightly warm left. Once you are satisfied the fire is out and all the embers are cold, then cover the area back over with the turf and undergrowth that was there before. The final satisfaction of your wild baking session is to look back at the spot where you so recently created a special place, where you used, enjoyed and shared the benefits of a fire, and realise that no one would ever know you'd been there. Was it all a dream?

How to build a campfire

Cooking in the wild is no fun without the fire. By all means learn how to start a fire from scratch by rubbing sticks, but unless you're a pro, don't attempt this while your friends are glaring hungrily at you.

Once you have decided what you want to cook and read the recipe, you'll have a better idea of the kind of fire you're going to need. Some fires require digging a hole first, others require large stones to reflect the heat, and flat stones for baking on. Time and energy spent at this stage will really pay off when it's time to serve up. It's much better to be prepared, which means taking all the right kit with you.

My 'go to' fire building technique is: having cleared a space, I start with the tinder, scrunched up paper or birch bark. Then scout-style, I make a teepee of kindling around and above the tinder, leaving a gap I can push my hand through for lighting. Finally, I add a few larger sticks or split logs that will easily catch – also in a teepee fashion. With a stack of dry wood to one side, I light the fire, blowing it into life and adding more fuel as required.

Lighter

I tend to use the brass zippo I bought when I was 14, but I recommend that you always take two lighters – and keep them separate. I also love the packs of strike-anywhere non-safety matches that I imagine I could use on my stubble. At home, I have a kitchen blowtorch that starts any fire sharpish. And in my survival kit, I have a magnifying

glass that on a sunny day, I've used to channel the sun's rays to start my fire. Very satisfying.

Tinder

Needless to say you need something to get your fire started. It's kinda like packing your passport when you go abroad: don't forget it! Keep some paper in a waterproof container that you can scrunch up and use to start a fire. Cotton wool also works a treat. The bark of silver birch is really resinous and great for starting fires – it will catch with a match and give enough heat to start most fires. Look out for some, and keep a bit in your pack.

Kindling

Kindling – small bits of dry wood – is essential to get your fire going. Keep a stash close to hand, because kindling is useful when you need a quick boost of heat or if your fire is close to going out. Some of the best wood can be found hanging in trees; if it's off the ground it can be much drier and easier to light and burn.

Fuel

Wood is the obvious choice, but it might not always be possible to find. In a nutshell, if you're at the beach look for driftwood; if you're up a mountain, chances are you'll have to get out your gas stove. For cooking and baking, you rarely need bits of wood thicker than your wrist. The dryer the wood the better; if it's damp or wet it will be hard to burn, will produce more smoke and the burning temperature will be lower.

Firewood stacked too tightly will not burn well. It's the spaces in-between that allow air to circulate and feed the fire. Great big logs are good for keeping the fire going into the night for warmth and a flicker of light.

Charcoal gets a fire really hot and is a useful back-up anywhere. An eco-disposable barbecue is a handy thing to keep in the boot of your car or by your back door for your next adventure. Basically it's a large hollowed-out log filled with sustainably made charcoal – just as easy to light and use as the metal ones but without the nasty lighter fuel taint on your food (and it won't end up in landfill afterwards).

Big logs at night, small wood in the morning

If last thing at night you place a couple of hefty bits of wood onto your fire, there's a chance the fire will still be going in the morning. Then in the morning add some small sticks, give it a blow (see technique below) and watch it crackle back to life. Burning smaller pieces of wood in the morning means that the fire will burn down more quickly, making it easier to put out and cover your tracks so you can leave no trace.

The Blow Diamond Technique

My good friend Tomas taught me the 'blow diamond' trick, picked up on a trip to Canada in his youth. Put the tips of your index fingers together in front of your face, and the tips of your thumbs together underneath. Push the fingers together to make a small diamond. Blow through this and with a little practice, you'll create a little horizontal tornado (see photo on next page). This is useful if the bit of the fire that needs encouragement is not very accessible, if you've an elaborate and flammable headpiece on, or like me you get asthma and too much smoke is liable to set you off.

Cooking outdoors

When you're cooking or baking in the wild, the campfire is far from the only option. Personally, I'm not a fan of a disposable barbecue simply because anything disposable seems wasteful and at odds with the spirit of wild baking. However, some companies make small portable barbecues that are easy enough to carry with you. My favourite is a shoebox-sized one made by Weber that goes and goes with only the smallest amount of fuel.

My son Milo has a jet boil: a small, neat, gas-powered stove that can boil anything up in top speed. This little device, and other similar ones, are perfect when fuel is scarce and carrying weight is a real consideration. Definitely one for the mountains.

8 Fires

There are many different ways to cook on a fire. In the index at the back, the recipes have been grouped by ingredient *and* cooking method so you can select a recipe according to the food and fire that you have.

1. **On a stick**
2. **On the embers**
3. **In the ash**
4. **On a flat hot stone**
5. **Hot stones under and above**
6. **Grill**
7. **Under the ground**
8. **In a pot**

On a stick

This is the most incidental and child-friendly way of cooking. For most of us it started as a marshmallow on the end of stick dangled over fire. This method also works well with sausages run through their entire length (use a slim, strong, smooth stick – see page 89). A most primitive form of unleavened bread is made by wrapping the dough around a stick and baking it over an open fire (see page 64). If you use a stick thick enough so that you can replace the stick with a sausage once the bread is cooked, you've got yourself a wild sausage roll, or hot dog extraordinaire. Just add a dollop of sauce and dunk it in some innuendo for an unforgettable evening. At the other end of the scale, it's entirely possible to roast a whole chicken on the end of the large stick propped above a fire.

On the embers

Some foods totally lend themselves to being dropped or placed directly on the embers. The second recipe in this book is for Ash-baked Sourdough Flatbreads (see page 57) where the dough is literally placed on top of the embers to bake. Mussels (see page 101) and other shellfish can also be cooked in this way without the need for a pan or a pot. The food takes on the essence of the fire in a way that is both simple and incomparable in flavour.

Ember farming, a term coined by Al Humphreys, is advanced fire prodding, the art of raking embers around to create hot zones and cooler areas for cooking on. Thin-ish sticks are stacked up on one side of the fire and burn to become your next batch of embers as they fall down into the bed of the fire. Ember farming is a hot and hugely rewarding part of the wild baking experience.

In the ash

Foods that have their own crust or skin can simply be pushed deep into the ash to bake to perfection. Australian bush-style damper bread (see page 70), jacket potatoes, baked squash, or why not a whole pumpkin, can be left to bake in all their glorious steaming earthy goodness.

On a flat hot stone

Once the fire has burned down and you're left with hot glowing embers, a flat stone placed on top of them can become the cooking surface for any number of glorious foods. This is essentially a primitive chef's plate and is ideal for things that need to be cooked on a dry heat. Think chapatti, bacon or delicious cheese toasties – or simply use to warm croissants.

When selecting your stones make sure they aren't the type that explode when heated. If in doubt check it out, either by looking it up online, or do what I did and encourage your wife's sister to marry a geologist. If you don't have far to travel you may find that taking a pizza or baking stone with you is a simple and safe option. The more oily and black the stone becomes over time, the better its functionality.

Hot stones under and above

The flat hot stone often needs to work in conjunction with a lid: a surface to reflect heat back down onto the food baking underneath. One way of achieving this is to put a few stones around the large flat stone, forming something of a wall and then placing an even larger flat stone on top of that. This lid can be heated in the fire before being placed on top, turning your hob into an oven. The first TV show I ever made solo was called *In Search of a Perfect Loaf* (BBC4). While filming, I visited a living history archaeological site in Cornwall where we built a bank oven in much the same way and placed a loaf inside that was in a glazed terracotta bowl. We covered the lot with clods of earth and pieces of turf to trap as much of the heat inside as possible. As you can imagine, the bread (which was made with elderberries) was earthy and delicious stuff. This method is useful for baking anything from pizza to cakes.

Grill

In essence this is your basic barbecue, a metal grill set above hot embers, for grilling meat, fish and veg. If your set-up is robust enough you can also use it to heat pans, for a less direct form of cooking. It's also not a bad way to keep things warm.

Under the ground

This is an ancient way of cooking large quantities of food. Variations of this method are found all over the world, including the Fijian *iovo*, the Hawaiian *luau* and the Māori *hāngi*. In essence, a large pit is dug into the ground and lined with stones, rocks and boulders to absorb the heat from the fire that is built in the pit. Once the fire has died down, wrapped food is placed on a layer of edible insulating vegetation that also goes on top of the food. This is done to trap the steam and flavours inside, while keeping ash and detritus from the fire from contaminating the food. Hot coals and ash are then placed on top to cook the food from above and trap the heat inside.

Large joints of meat or even whole animals can be cooked this way and majestically pulled from the ground – cooked to perfection and having absorbed the flavours of all the other ingredients. Herbs, spices, vegetables and the earth itself all meld together while life continues above the ground.

For a celebratory gathering of people in the wild, I can think of no better way to prepare the food. The un-earthing ceremony is simply magical. I've only done this a handful of times and each time the suspense of waiting to see how the food comes out has dramatically added to the sense of occasion. For my brother-in-law Rufus's 40th birthday we baked 10kg of beef brisket this way. Everyone gathered round as we dug it out of the ground, the smell was awesome and everyone agreed, it was the finest damn beef that they had ever eaten.

In a pot

A sturdy pot with a good lid, like a Dutch oven (pictured opposite), is a heavy and wonderful thing to cook with. A robust one can be placed directly on the fire or even in the fire with embers sitting on the lid for an all-over bake. A good Dutch oven can also be suspended from a tripod above the fire for slow-cooked casseroles or soups. This is the home of the One Pot Wonder (more of this to follow). It's also an excellent way to bake your sourdough bread.

Front cover of the book to this page is the ideal pitta dough thickness! (see page 63)

Anyone can bake

—

Grandpa Herbert

First and foremost I'm into bread. The recipes that
follow have been in my family for generations and
are a constant companion whenever we cook outside.
Every recipe in this book, in every location, will have
an accompanying bread so if you're flour frigid get over
yourself and hug your inner baker. Your friends and
family will love you for it.

All of these recipes can be baked at home so you have
the option to practise, freeze ahead of time, and take
with you.

---

15 steps to making better bread

1. **Allow enough time for baking.** And remember that mostly the dough will be resting.

2. **Preparation is everything.** Read the recipe through and check, check, check that you've got the right kit and ingredients.

3. **Don't be a flour floozie.** All flours are not the same. Find a good flour and stick with it.

4. **If you can mill your own flour, do it.** It's better (see page 20).

5. **Risen bread is best.** Use baking powder if you're in a hurry; otherwise yeast (fresh or dry), sourdough starter or fermented water will all give you a rise. More about that coming up.

6. **Slower is better.** If you have time use wild yeasts in your sourdough starter or fermented water to get good bugs into your bread and then into your biodome.

7. **Knead your dough enough.** Giving your dough a work-out develops the gluten and makes your dough more stretchy. This allows the dough to rise and hold its shape. Or, don't knead it, keep it in the fridge or somewhere cool and fold the dough every couple of hours to slowly develop its elasticity – this is the no-knead method.

8. **You can weigh your water:** 1ml water weighs 1g. One litre water weighs 1kg.

9. **When baking on or in a fire**, the thinner or smaller the dough piece, the more likely it'll be baked on the inside

before it burns on the outside. If it does start to burn before it's baked, tin foil is your friend. Use it as a field dressing to reflect heat away from the burning area.

10. **The temperature of the water** will affect how quickly or slowly your dough rises. You might want to use cold water to make a dough that rises slowly overnight. If you use warm water, the yeast or starter works more quickly to rise your dough. Yeast will perish above 55°c so don't heat your water too much.

11. **Keep your sourdough starter warm** by taking it to bed with you, like the San Franciscan gold prospectors of old.

12. **When making the dough**, keep your sourdough starter or yeast separate from the salt until you're ready to mix.

13. **Wetter is better.** When making a dough, it's easier to slowly add flour as you need – and knead – it.

14. **If your dough is too wet**, add a little more flour.

15. **If your dough is too dry**, add a little more water.

Measurements 101

Being the eldest of my grandpa Herbert's 18 grandchildren I heard him pose this riddle many times: 'Which is heavier, a sack with a tonne of coal in, or a sack with a tonne of feathers?' Okay, so we know they both weigh the same and the feathers must be in a ginormous sack, so what if the receptacle or cup you use for measuring is always the same one?

I've been a fan of digital scales since breaking away from the old imperial brass weight ones of my college days but when it comes to wild baking, I've seen the wisdom of using cups to measure ingredients. It's less of a faff than packing scales, plus a single cup is light, portable and easy to include in your kit. So to help you visualise a cup and what it can equal in terms of weight, here goes.

1 cup filled to the top or the fill line will yield:
— 280g sourdough starter
— 240g/ml water (or other liquid)
— 200g grain / sugar / dried fruit
— 120g flour (equals two hands cupped together)
— 110g oats

If you don't already own a set of American-style measuring cups, it's worth finding one to have as part of your wild baking kit – choose one that's reasonably robust. Weigh or measure 240g/ml water using digital scales at home, pour into your chosen cup and mark off the fill line on the cup (ideally it would be full to the brim).

In time you'll become more aware of the *mass* of ingredients: water being heavier than flour. Freshly milled flour is particularly light and fluffy.

I believe that recipes are far easier to memorise and share this way too, and using cups kicks against the fussy and exacting stigma that baking has attracted recently. As your cup and the various ingredients weighed in it become more familiar, it becomes part of a looser style of cooking and baking. This frees up capacity to focus on texture and flavour. Truly a more enjoyable way to bake.

Measurements 101 done, now charge your cup and raise it for me, will ya? Cheers!

Temperature 101

Flippin' HOT (240–350°C / 460–660°F)
— Flour dusted onto the surface burns quickly!
— Not really possible to put your hands too near this heat for longer than two seconds
— Ideal for quick and thin things on a grill or stone: searing steak, pizzas, flatbreads, pittas
— Use long tongs
— Long, buttoned-up cotton sleeves

HOT (200–240°C / 390–460°F)
— Flour dusted onto a surface will slowly go golden
— Ideal for baking most loaves

HOT-ish (160–200°C / 320–390°F)
— Say goodbye to your soggy bottom when baking on a stone
— Ideal for slow cooking and cakes

Now things are hotting up around here, it's time to get our bake on!

Sourdough Bread

We've got to think of a better name for this bread. Yes it tastes sour, but it is so, so, so much more than this. It's wonderfully cyclical – a never-ending process, handed down from generation to generation, a way of life. It is the original and best way of rising bread, going back to the ancients, when prior to this all breads were unleavened. And what do we call this mighty life-giving thing? Sourdough bread.

So what makes sourdough bread so great?

1. It can be made with just three ingredients: flour, water and salt. So no commercial yeast.

2. When flour and water are mixed together, after a few days and with the right conditions (food, water, oxygen, warmth), it will start to ferment. The wild yeasts in the air, and on the flour, find this wet mixture the perfect environment, converting the starches in the flour into carbon dioxide. In time, this becomes the bubbles in sourdough bread. Add to this the lively lactobacillus, that also makes its home in the 'starter', not only feeding our gut in the most extraordinary way, but also gives sourdough bread it's wonderful sour tang.

3. Given the right conditions when wild baking (a hot 'oven' with a bit of steam, a wet enough dough), sourdough bread develops a delicious crust as it bakes that helps trap moisture inside and slows down the staling (drying out) process in the most natural way. Sourdough naturally keeps for a long time.

4. The long, slow fermentation not only gives the bread a wonderful flavour, it also makes it easier to digest for the many people who struggle with soft, fluffy factory bread.

5. A sourdough starter, if fed correctly, could live for ever. BOOM! Who are you going to leave yours to in your will? Sounds freaky? My late grandfather fed the starter my brothers and I are now custodians of. It's over 60 years old.

6. You can grow your sourdough starter, infinitely! You can share your starter with all your friends, and everyone you will ever meet, baking all the bread the world will ever need. There's a great challenge!

How to make a sourdough starter 🏠

First, source some flour. Option 1 is to find a mill, ideally local to you, that produces stoneground organic dark rye flour (search online if you don't already know of one). Buy a small bag. Option 2 goes a step further: for your next birthday, encourage everyone to club together to buy you a tiny stoneground mill for your kitchen. Then visit your local mill and buy a small bag of cleaned organic rye *grain* and mill the flour fresh and as required.

Thoroughly clean a large jar with a lid for keeping your sourdough starter in – a Kilner jar is ideal. It's worthwhile at this stage to weigh your empty jar, and make a note of this on an address label stuck to the jar or on a tag tied round the top. This will help you to know exactly how much sourdough starter is in your jar at any one time without having to empty it out.

Day 1

Weigh 75g warm water and 75g dark rye flour into your jar.
Using a fork or small whisk give it a mix. Put the lid on.
Leave the jar somewhere warm to start the fermentation.

Days 2, 3, 4, 5

Repeat the mixing and storing process.

By now you'll have noticed a few bubbles appearing, like
the first windy smiles of a baby.

By my reckoning you'll have more than enough starter to
start baking sourdough bread. This young starter will rise
your bread, now the wild yeast is established, and in time
(about 3 months), it will develop a wonderful flavour, as
the *lactobacillus* also becomes established.

As you can imagine this is a great thing to do with the kids.
They can have their very own pet monster to feed. Which
leads me to the next thing – naming it. Our Hobbs House
Bakery family starter is called 'The Monster', but call yours
what you will: 'Mother', 'Belcher', 'Tom', whatever you feel.
Go wild, have a naming ceremony, wet the baby's head,
whatever, but be sure to let me know.

Should you need any advice or encouragement, please feel
free to join the lively community on Facebook, search for
Sourdough Nation Public Group.

Fermented water

This can be used to raise bread instead of sourdough starter or yeast (though it'll take longer than adding yeast). I use mine in addition to the sourdough starter because I love the extra complexity of flavour and deliciousness it adds to my bread.

Pick a handful of something edible from your garden – rosemary is my favourite but other herbs, rose hips and edible berries can also be good – and put into a sterilised 1 litre jar with a sealable lid. Half-fill with filtered water. Add 3 heaped tablespoons of sugar (I prefer golden caster but muscovado is good and adds a rich, warm flavour to your bread).

Keep the jar at warm room temperature (24-ish°c). Shake it morning and night for 4 days – just a quick shake every time you pass it. Give it a taste on day 4; it may already be starting to fizz. That's good. Now add more filtered water until the jar is four-fifths full, and add another 3 tablespoons of sugar.

Shake, shake, shake for 5 more days. Your water should now be fermenting, and no longer be sweet as the wild yeasts do their work. Now you can keep the jar in the fridge for several months until you need it. To reactivate, add more sugar and shake. After each bout of shaking, open it and release any gas to prevent a build up.

The fermented water is good to go when it's fizzing (especially after a shake) and not sweet. Whatever you take out of the jar can be replaced with fresh garden edibles and water. If ever it smells or tastes bad, ditch it and start again.

I have found fermented rosemary water, served over ice on a hot day, is a beautiful and refreshing pro-biotic drink. The West Country's answer to kombucha?

Credit for this technique must go to PPG Baker Pablo, with whom I spent a few days in Germany at Mock Mill, the home of freshly-milled flour.

Sourdough-it-all 🏠

It's not a bad idea to get this mighty loaf going when you make your evening meal. Give it its final shape before putting it aside for its last rise as you sleep. In the morning, having stoked your fire, your loaf will be ready to bake. Using cold water and a longer rise lowers the temperature of the dough and therefore the yeast activity; a slower rise = better flavour, so you can start your day in the very best wild baking way.

This recipe makes a big batch of dough: do as we did and divide the dough into three once it's mixed together to make any combination of the following:

Loaf – all of the dough
Pitta @ 100g each (big hen-sized egg)
Pizza @ 150–200g each (goose egg)
Bagels @ 80g each (small egg)
Doughnuts @ 40g each (tiny songbird egg)

MAKES: *1 large loaf*
TAKES: *6½–12 hours (including resting)*
KIT: *cup, large mixing bowl, shower cap, dough scraper, oven glove, chopping board, Dutch oven, heavy pan with lid, or a flat baking stone*

—

4 cups strong white bread flour, plus extra for dusting
1 cup (280g) sourdough starter
1 cup hot or cold water (or fermented water)
Big pinch (10g) of sea salt

Add the ingredients to a bowl and mix together. For a really open-textured bread you can autolyse the dough. This means holding back the salt at the start and keeping the dough very soft (just the right side of sticky). This allows it to develop, giving you a stretchier dough. After the dough has rested for 1 hour, add the salt and work it through.

Again, only add more water or flour if you're really sure you need it.

No skimping on the kneading. Take it slow for a full 15 minutes or, if you're going at it like the clappers, give it 10.

Once your dough is smooth and soft, put it back in the bowl, cover and leave it somewhere warm to rise for 2 hours (or 1 more hour if you've been autolysing).

After that, take your dough out and shape it on a very lightly floured surface and pop into a basket or tin. Cover and leave somewhere warm to rise. If you've used hot water this will need 4 hours' rising. If you wish to rise it overnight to bake first thing in the morning, then leave it somewhere cool, even in the fridge. This is called retarding and can yield you an even tastier, more open crumb loaf. What you want to avoid is a loaf that is over-risen and collapses in the oven. If your loaf has been in a fridge for 8 hours it will likely need a couple of hours outside to warm up and rise before baking. My personal preference is to wait until it is nearly risen enough before putting it into the fridge to be retarded. This way it can typically go from the fridge to the oven the moment your oven is hot enough.

Bake your bread (ideally on a baking stone or in a Dutch oven) at 240°C with a good steam until golden. This can take up to 35 minutes but it's wise to check it after 20 and turn the loaf around (especially if practising at home with a fan oven) and let the steam out. Also it's a good idea to notch the temperature down to about 210°C after 15 minutes. Starting off hot gives a good 'oven spring'; lowering the heat gives a thorough bake throughout. If baking in a Dutch oven on a tripod over a fire, you can raise or lower it to adjust the temperature. To check it's fully baked hold the loaf with a dry cloth or glove and tap it on the bottom. If it sounds hollow, it's baked!

Life Loaf 🏠

Once you are satisfied with your basic sourdough loaf, it's time to try blending different grains and flours, noticing the different tastes. Now we're milling in the Herbert house we're loving the way that long fermentation, freshly milled flour and fermented water all come together to make a tasty and fibrous loaf. This ticks all the boxes, hence the name.

MAKES: *1 small loaf (approx. 500g)*
TAKES: *6½ hours*
KIT: *as previous recipe*
—

1 cup wholemeal wheat bread flour, plus extra for dusting
1 cup (125g) spelt
½ cup (140g) sourdough starter
½ cup (120g) warm water (or fermented water, page 52)
Pinch (5g) of sea salt

Mix all the ingredients together and knead.
Cover and rest for 2 hours.
Shape the loaf, roll in kibbled toasted barley or seeds.
Cover and rest for 4 hours.
Bake at 230°c for 20 minutes or until golden.

Tips
— *Ideal baked in a small tin.*
— *Also ideal for baking under embers – no tin! See Bush Damper (page 70) for method.*
— *Try adding pre-soaked healthy seeds into the dough: linseed, chia, sunflower all work well – half a cup covered with water and left overnight to soak.*

Ash-baked Sourdough Flatbreads

These beauties were my first foray into baking outside; my freedom from the tyranny of scales and precision. They were also my ticket to the Do Lectures back in 2010. We'd been baking them in the embers of the wood-fired oven at our bistro at the back of Hobbs House Bakery in Nailsworth. Ant Smith, the chef, served them up with his awesome hanger steak, and we loved them. So I suggested running an Ash-baked Sourdough Flatbreads workshop in the woods at the Do Lectures, and they said yes.

This recipe, out of all of my recipes, is the one that forced me to look at the entire breadmaking process anew. When I was baking in the woods I found it so liberating not to have scales, but to rely on taste and touch and to make bread with nothing more than a bowl, a campfire and 25 willing Doers. 'Russian Bob' kept me plied with ale and 'Evil Gordon' was my overqualified lackey (he now helps to run BeerBods – check it out). Together we made a trough full of chewy and delicious flatbreads. We took them through the trees back to the Bothy where we met Darina Allen of Ballymaloe Cookery School. Her group of Doers had made lemon curd, warm and irresistible in its massive pan. Fifty of us tore into the bread, dipped it into the warm lemon curd under a Welsh sky full of stars and people fell in love. Baking can do this.

It's much easier to bake these in daylight. If not, you'll need a good lamp or similar so you can see what's baking. Either that or a keen sense of smell.

MAKES: *8*

TAKES: *1 hour*

FIRE: *burned down to a good bed of glowing embers*

KIT: *mixing bowl, shower cap, dough scraper, penknife, small pan, thermometer, tea towel, tongs, chopping board (optional)*

**4 cups wholemeal or white bread flour, plus extra
for dusting
Big pinch of sea salt
1 cup (280g) sourdough starter (or use 10g fresh yeast
or 5g dried yeast)
1 cup (240g/ml) water, ideally warmed in a pan to
30–40°C, plus extra for perfecting the dough**

Light your fire and while it's burning make the dough.

First, mix all the ingredients together in your mixing bowl.
Work the dough for 15 minutes until it's smooth and elastic,
only adding extra flour or water if you're sure it's needed.
The dough should be soft but not too sticky. Cover the bowl
of dough with a shower cap and leave it to rest and rise for
30–60 minutes, somewhere warm, like near your fire.

While it rises prepare a good bed of hot embers. The larger the
embers the less ash dust you'll have on the flatbreads.

Cut off a small plum-sized bit of dough, roll it in lightly
floured hands and then pat it between your hands to flatten
it. Slowly and carefully tease the dough out as round and flat
as you can make it without tearing. Squeeze and pinch any
larger, thicker bits of dough and pinch closed any holes that
appear. And if the dough sticks too much, dust it with a little
flour. A tea towel is useful for keeping hands clean and free of
too much dough. Repeat with the remaining dough.

Carefully place the raw breads directly on to the embers and
watch them bake. They might puff up a bit with some good air
bubbles – that's the moisture in the dough turning to steam
and being trapped in the stretchy dough you've made. Lovely.

Keep an eye on them – a bit of char is good but make sure
they don't burn too much. Once they are golden underneath –
after about 3–5 minutes – use your tongs or two sticks to flip
them over and bake on the other side.

Remove the baked flatbreads from the embers and use a penknife or a stick to flick off any baked-in embers. Keep your flatbreads warm in a tea towel or on a log above the fire. I tend to bake these two at a time. That way, not so many embers are needed and it's easier to keep an eye on them.

These are perfect eaten warm and will make an ideal side for stews and dips, soaking up beer, you name it. They definitely make eating outside that bit tastier.

Tip
— *You can make the dough at home using cold water to slow the rising down. Take it with you in a sealed plastic container big enough to allow the dough to at least double in size.*

Pizza 🏠

The ingredients and method for this pizza dough is the same as for the Ash-baked Sourdough Flatbreads, so refer to the previous recipe to make the dough, adding a good glug of olive oil when mixing the ingredients together.

> MAKES: *4 large or 8 small*
> TAKES: *5 hours (including 4 hours' resting)*
> FIRE: *burned down to a good bed of glowing embers*
> KIT: *big flat stone to cook on, lid, rolling pin (use a wine bottle or unopened can of beer), dough scraper*

Once you've made the dough, leave it to rise in the bowl for 4 hours. Every hour use your dough scraper to turn the dough – this involves pushing your scraper down the inside of the bowl and under the dough to release it, then pull the top edge of the dough over the top surface and then push it down, knocking out some of the air in the process. Work your way around the bowl half a dozen times: scraping › stretching › folding › pushing, to further develop the strength of the dough. This way you'll get a superb stretchy dough for the pizza bases and an irresistible sour flavour.

After 4 hours your dough will be ready. On your chopping board divide the dough into 4 equal pieces (or 8 if you want small pizzas – they are easier to make in the wild) and shape them into balls. Cover and leave to rest for 10 minutes.

Put your large flat stone onto the embers so it gets really hot. You'll also need a lid – try an inverted pan – to reflect the heat onto the top to melt the cheese.

Right then, working with one ball at a time, and with plenty of dusting flour to hand, pat the dough flat. When you've got it evenly round and half as big as your palm, then you need to get it flat. Either roll it out or throw it with a flick of your wrists using both sets of knuckles. DO NOT drop it in the dirt.

Once you've achieved your desired thickness and made sure you have plenty of flour underneath, add the topping. It's pizza, you know what to do. Nevertheless, here are some tips:

— Leave a clean rim around your base; toppings that fall into the fire burn and waft acrid smoke in your face.

— Thin tomato (or bianca) layer first, then cheese, then toppings.

— Less is more. A pizza piled high will not cook properly without burning underneath and hogging the stone.

Place the pizza onto a baking stone and leave to cook for 3–5 minutes. Remove carefully. You can also do this in an oven turned up as hot as it will go.

Finish is everything. After baking, drizzle on oil, season, grate on Parmesan, add fresh herbs.

Pitta Breads 🏠

Once again, refer to the recipe for Ash-baked Sourdough Flatbreads to make the dough.

MAKES: *8 pitta breads*
TAKES: *1 hour*
FIRE: *burned down to a good bed of glowing embers*
KIT: *big flat stone to cook on, lid, rolling pin (use a wine bottle or unopened can of beer)*

Make the dough as before and let it rest for 30 minutes while you heat your flat stone in the embers.

Divide the dough into 8 pieces, shape into rounds and rest for a couple of minutes before rolling out on a very well-floured chopping board. The more evenly you can roll them out, the higher your chances of pitta perfection. About 3–4 mm thick is good (or use this book as a guide, front cover to page 40!)

Place them on top of your very hot flat stone and cover with something that reflects the heat well. After just 30 seconds you'll notice the dough starts to blister. This part is truly wondrous – as the blisters grow and join others, so the pitta rises from the stone as if alive – one tremendous bubble of delicious dough, a steamy pocket of joy. As soon as the pitta starts to show any sign of colour from baking, after about 1–2 minutes, whip it off and leave to collapse and cool for a minute or two.

These are best eaten fresh the same day – being so thin they dry out quite quickly and become flaky. Perfect for dipping into juicy delicious things and ace in a salad. Or just enjoy with butter.

Tip
— *At home: turn up oven as hot as it will go and bake on a pre-heated baking stone*

Snobrød

Aka Twist Bread, Stick Bread, Campfire Bread, Bread Snakes.

> MAKES: *1 per stick*
> TAKES: *about 5 minutes to bake*
> FIRE: *burned down to a good bed of glowing embers*
> KIT: *1 long straight stick per bread*

Each person making bread needs to find a long straight stick and clean it up for baking. The thicker your stick, the bigger your hole so the more filling options you'll have (although it will take slightly longer to bake).

Use the recipe for Ash-baked Sourdough Flatbreads on page 57 to make the dough. Once it's had its half-hour rest, lightly dust your hands with flour, twist off a small handful of dough and roll the dough out between your hands until you have a stick-shaped sausage of dough. Coil it tightly around your stick, taking care not to tear it and leaving no gaps. Hold your stick over the hot embers, twizzling it occasionally until it's baked, and voilà! Snobrød!

Once it's cooled for a few moments, tease your bread off the stick, fill, dip and devour.

Wanna proper wild Hot Dog? See page 89.

Sourdough Bagels 🏠

Say wha?! Bagels done on a campfire? Well, you better believe it! If you're chilling outside and are hungry to impress *and* you like a big breakfast *and* you love bagels, then this one's for you.

I've made this outside on several occasions, once at The Good Life Experience in front of a marquee packed full of lovely and curious people. I was kneading the dough and my Madonna-style microphone slipped. Quick as you like, Jeremy Vine himself leapt to my rescue. Cheers Jez, have a bagel.

BREAD

MAKES: *8 big bagels*
TAKES: *1 hour, plus 10 hours' rising*
SPEED OPTION: *1 hour in total*
KIT: *2 Dutch ovens (or 1 big pan and a Dutch oven), large mixing bowl, shower cap (or clingfilm), dough scraper, pastry brush (what, camping? I'd use a small bunch of rosemary or the tail of a willing squirrel), chopping board, slotted spoon (you might get away with a few clean tent pegs)*

—

4 cups (480g) strong bread flour, plus extra for dusting
½ cup (140g) sourdough starter (see page 50)
Speed option: If you want to make these quickly then
    also add a 1 inch (2.5cm) cube of fresh yeast (15g)
    or 1 × 7g sachet of dried yeast
1 cup warm water
2 glugs oil
Good pinch (6g) of sea salt
1 generous tsp honey or maple syrup
1 egg, separated
1 tbsp poppy seeds

Put all the ingredients including the egg white but *excluding* the egg yolk and poppy seeds into your bowl. Using your dough scraper, mix the ingredients together until there are no dried lumps then knead and work the dough for 10 minutes until it's well developed, smooth and stretchy. Cover and leave to rest for 1 hour (20 minutes if you're taking the speed option).

Tip the risen dough out onto your lightly floured chopping board and cut it into 8 equal pieces. First shape each one into a round, then make a big (carrot thickness) hole in the middle using a floured finger or thumb. And get wanging (the technical term for spinning a hole on your floured digit). Place your bagels on the now well-floured chopping board, leaving a little space for them to rise, and cover. Leave for 8–9 hours (20 minutes if you're speeding up). In other words, go to bed.

In the morning stoke your fire; boil up a large pan of water and heat up your Dutch oven until it's quite hot. Carefully lower your bagels – 2 to 4 at a time – into the boiling water and watch as they bob to the surface. I ain't gonna lye (bagel geek joke) this is my favourite part. After 60 seconds, turn the bagels over and give them another minute before removing and placing them back onto the board.

Next, very carefully brush your bagels with the egg yolk and sprinkle on the poppy seeds. Bake them in the Dutch oven (at 200-ish°c) for 20 minutes or until golden, delicious and baked.

Alternatively bake on a hot stone over embers with an inverted pan on top. Make sure they don't burn, especially underneath. Check them regularly and if they start to burn lift them off the bottom of the oven with either some scrunched-up foil, a stack of (non-toxic) leaves or a couple of beer mats.

Try these bagels with hot smoked salmon (see page 137).

Options
— *Make the dough at home, chill it in the fridge and take it with you.*
— *Bake your bagels at home, take with you, toast over the fire.*

Beer Bread 🏠

No knead. No rise. Super-quick. This cheeky li'l loaf is fast and flexible. With its non-perishable ingredients, this is the ideal bake for the end of a long wilderness trip when you're in need of a homely, comforting bread and minimal washing-up!

MAKES: *1 large loaf*
TAKES: *45 minutes*
FIRE: *a good bed of hot coals*
KIT: *big mixing bowl, wooden spoon, chopping board, Dutch oven or large skillet with a lid, tongs (or hunting knife) for turning the bread over during baking, dough scraper, infrared thermometer*

—

3½ cups flour, plus extra for dusting
Pinch (6g) of sea salt
1 heaped tsp baking powder
1 × 330ml bottle beer (something crafty), plus 1 for
**   yourself while the loaf is baking**
2 glugs oil

First, set your pan or Dutch oven to gently heat above the fire.

Mix the dry ingredients together by hand in a large bowl.

In your bowl mix the beer and the oil into the dry ingredients until there are no dry lumps. The mixture should be very sticky and tacky but firm enough to stay in the bowl when turned upside-down. Think DIY crack filler.

Now dust the chopping board generously with the dusting flour. Plop all the dough out onto the floured board. Flour your hands and flip the dough so it is dusted top and bottom with flour. Then cup the damp dough and round it into a pleasing shape. Cut the dough through with a cross (in honour of the traditional Irish soda bread): it'll also bake quicker and make 4 handy batched rolls. Carefully lift the dough into the hot pan or Dutch oven and put the lid on, adding some embers on top if you can (the pan should ideally be 210–230°C).

Bake for 15–20 minutes or until it has started to form a good golden crust that sounds hollow when tapped on the bottom. If black smoke wafts out (and you smell burnt toast), it is indeed starting to burn. If it has had less than 10 minutes, it's too hot and you should raise the pan and flip the loaf over.

> **Note**
> *Want to save your beer for drinking? Make the*
> *Homemade Butter recipe on page 79 and use the*
> *uncultured buttermilk and enough milk to make the*
> *total amount needed, along with a squeeze of lemon.*

Optional Extras
Check the beer bottle label for any hints to its flavour and pimp your bread with those things. So a beer with a zesty finish and a mellow honey flavour and fruity aroma could inspire you to add some lemon zest, diced apple, raisins and a spoon of honey. Some of these will make the dough much wetter so compensate by adding less beer.

— Up to 100g of any seeds, ideally toasted over the fire
— Old bits of cheese that need using up
— Handful of dried fruit, big pieces chopped
— Handful of granola or muesli

Try foraging for these seasonal edibles and then add them to your bake: wild garlic, elderberries, blackberries, cobnuts, fennel seeds, samphire, sea purslane.

Bush Damper

This is the Australian way of baking in the ash of the fire – and it's super-rewarding.

Simply allow your fire to die down or clear it to one side. Hollow out a just-big-enough 'oven' and place your rounded dough in it (when shaping the loaf, flatten it to about wrist-thickness). Then cover with ash and then some hot embers and leave to bake for 30 minutes. Dig up your loaf, knock off the ash and tap it on the bottom; if it sounds hollow then it's baked. Pop it back for a further 10 minutes if you're not sure. If you'd rather avoid traces of ash in your diet, wrap the loaf in foil before baking.

Also an ideal method for baking spuds, squash, small pumpkins, etc.

Cornbread 'n' Cheese

My first experience of this was at the Four Roses Bourbon distillery and it is a worthy wild baking contender. It's quick to make (raised as it is with baking powder), it's superb at soaking up juicy stews, casseroles and hot sauce and it's relatively easy to bake. Also a square of this on the side of a steaming bowl of Burgoo Stew (see page 123) brings the carbs like nothing else.

MAKES: *enough for 6 as a side*
TAKES: *35 minutes*
FIRE: *hot stone propped above embers*
KIT: *big piece of baking parchment, shallow foil tray (slightly bigger than A5), mixing bowl, whisk, small pan*

—

1 cup cornmeal, plus extra for dusting
½ cup plain flour
1 tbsp baking powder
4 big finger pinches of salt, plus extra for topping
3 tbsp sweetness (sugar, honey, maple syrup)
100g butter
¼ tin (75g) sweetcorn
½ cup milk and natural yoghurt mixed together
2 eggs
Handful of grated (or chopped) mature Cheddar cheese
Optional toppings: slices of chilli, more grated cheese,
    lime zest, sliced red onion

Heat a stone propped above hot embers. The stone should be big enough to sit the roasting tray on to heat to 200°c.

Mix all the dry ingredients (except the cheese) together in the bowl. Melt the butter in the pan, then stir into the dry ingredients with the sweetcorn. Slowly whisk in the eggs, milk and yoghurt mix. Now for your workout. Whisk this all

BREAD

thoroughly together for 5 minutes until you have a lump free, thick batter.

Line the tray with baking parchment and dust the bottom with cornmeal for a wonderful crunch. Pour over half of the mixture. Scatter over the grated cheese and then add the rest of the mixture on top. Add any optional toppings.

Bake for 20 minutes or until golden all over, using a lid or something to reflect the heat from the fire onto the top of the cornbread. Five minutes into baking, finish with a sprinkle of sea salt flakes. To see if it's ready, insert a knife; if it comes out clean (save for a bit of cheese) the bread is baked.

HOT FAT CAUTION

The next recipes involve working with hot oil. This can be dangerous as oil is very flammable. Should the oil get too hot or if a bridge is created between the fire and the oil, a fat fire will start.

Do a risk assessment and make sure everyone in the vicinity knows you are about to start a high-risk recipe. Make sure there is nothing flammable near the pan of oil, that the fire itself is well established with calm hot embers and no risk of flare-up. Have the pan lid to hand along with some thick oven gloves. Check your thermometer is working properly. Never attempt this in an enclosed space where you could become trapped – NEVER IN A TENT. Check that there isn't anything flammable above the fire.

In the event of a fat fire, DO NOT THROW WATER ON IT. Alert everyone nearby and carefully replace the lid to starve the fire of oxygen. If you can, turn off the heat or safely remove the pan from the fire. Don't take any risks. Vacate the area until the fire has burnt itself out. If necessary call the emergency services.

Cheery Churros 🏠

I first made these in Laos with my son Milo under a big mango tree near the Thai border with a dozen young women. We went with Tearfund – a charity I'm an ambassador for – to teach pizza making. However, on day one we were told that no one there knew what pizza was – and they didn't have cheese. So Milo and I prayed for inspiration, went to the local food market and came up with these beauties. This recipe is as we shared it in Laos. We used the water bottle instead of scales and the cap from the bottle to measure the small ingredients.

Make sure you've read the HOT FAT CAUTION so you know how to deal with a fat fire.

MAKES: *12*

TAKES: *30 minutes*

KIT: *2 pans (one to be heavy-based and high-sided for deep-frying), mixing bowl, fork, good thermometer, tongs, kitchen paper*

—

2 cups (500ml) bottled water
2 glugs or tbsp olive or rapeseed oil
3 cups plain flour
1 cap (5g) salt
3 caps (20g) baking powder
5 caps (25g) sugar
1 litre vegetable oil
Caster sugar and orange zest, for dusting

Carefully heat your oil up to 170°C in the heavy-based pan, taking care to ensure it is stable.

Put the water and oil into the second pan and bring to the boil.

Mix the flour, salt, baking powder and sugar in a bowl. Slowly add the hot water mixture. Using a fork quickly mix in the water.

You should have a stiff, sticky dough – don't overwork it.

Once the oil is 170°c, dust your hands with flour and, working quickly with light hands, roll the dough into longish sticks. They should be about thumb thickness. The thicker they are the harder it will be to cook them right through.

Use a small bit of your dough to test the temperature of the oil. After a few seconds a little ball of dough should rise to the top of the oil from the bottom and after only a couple of minutes it should be golden. If it burns quickly or stays pale for ages, then adjust the temperature.

Working in small batches (frying too many at once will lower the temperature of the oil), carefully fry the churros in the hot oil, deliberately lowering them in away from you so if there is a splash of oil it's not on your face. They should take 3–5 minutes to become golden and crispy on the outside and fluffy in the middle. Lift out of the oil with tongs and drain on kitchen paper.

After a few seconds tip them onto a tray or plate of caster sugar and orange zest and roll them around to give them a frosting. Resist the temptation to eat them right away as they will burn your mouth.

Photo © Ralph Hodgson / Tearfund

Hot Chocolate Sauce

When we were walking in Laos, we turned a corner to see a humongous billboard promoting MILO Drinking Chocolate. It was a sign for sure. We bought some and mixed it with condensed milk for a delicious dunking sauce.

Alternatively, melt a knob of butter (in the pan you boiled the water in) then add a bar of dark chocolate (typically 100g) and the same amount of double cream. Add a teaspoon of sugar and a pinch of salt and melt over a gentle heat until you've a silky and irresistible chocolate sauce for dipping your churros in.

Campfire Hot Chocolate

Make the sauce as above and then dilute with milk until it's the perfect intensity. Take care not to burn or boil the chocolate. And *if* you can whisk it, then do, for a lump-free fluffy hot chocolate. We like to add toasted marshmallows on top of ours and let them melt into the drink. I – and some other people I know – like a dash of rum added in the end. Jus'sayin'.

Dangerous Sourdough Doughnuts

These campfire doughnuts risen with sourdough to give them
a tremendous flavour are a Do Lectures original from the
year 2015. They have been a real hit and worth the extra care
taken to ensure everything is safe. I've never seen a plate of
food so furiously demolished. Word about them spread like
wildfire throughout the camp and for the rest of the evening
people were asking me about them as if they were something
illegal: 'Mate/buddy/bro/bruv/fella/Tom, you got any of those
doughnuts left?' I didn't even have the hot chocolate sauce.

MAKES: *8 large or 16 small*
TAKES: *about 3 hours (including resting)*
KIT: *large heavy-based pan with a tight-fitting lid (a Dutch
oven is perfect), long metal tongs, mixing bowl, shower cap
or clingfilm, dough scraper, chopping board, roasting tray,
thermometer, thick oven gloves*

—

4 cups flour, plus extra for dusting
1 cup sourdough starter
1 cup warm milk
Pinch of sea salt
3 tbsp sugar, plus extra for coating
Big knob (50g) of butter
2 litres vegetable oil

Measure all of the ingredients into a bowl and mix together.
Work and knead the dough for 15 minutes or until your dough
is soft, smooth and elastic. Add more flour if your dough is
too sticky.

Now with your dough in the bowl cover it with clingfilm or a
shower cap and leave it to rest and rise somewhere warm for
2 hours (near the fire is good but do turn the bowl occasionally
so it doesn't bake on one side).

Pull out small, plum-sized pieces of dough and shape them as round as you can using only a small amount of flour for dusting. Line the doughnuts up on the board and keep covered and warm as before for about 45 minutes for their final rise.

Meanwhile preheat your oil to 165°C in a heavy-based pan. Cover with lid.

Carefully lower the doughnuts into the hot oil and fry for 3 minutes, then use the tongs to turn them over.

Give them 3 minutes on the other side until they are lovely and golden.

Put the sugar for coating into the roasting tray. As you carefully remove the doughnuts, immediately roll them in the sugar.

Leave to cool for a couple of minutes before devouring them.

BREAD

Tips
— *Add a teaspoon of ground cinnamon to the coating sugar.*
— *Make your doughnuts smaller (about the size of a date) so there are more to go around. They'll fry quicker too (2 minutes each side).*
— *These are superb with Hot Chocolate Sauce (see page 75).*

Dark Chocolate Banana Loaf Cake

My brother Henry made this for my birthday on a barbecue. With the addition of chocolate, we have here a killer cake.

MAKES: *6 large portions*
TAKES: *40 minutes*
KIT: *large foil baking tray or loaf tin, mixing bowl, whisk, wooden spoon, pan, flat baking stone heated to 180°C*

—

85g or big knob of butter
½ cup (100g) brown sugar
2 eggs
4 small ripe bananas (or 3 big ones)
1 bar (100g) good dark chocolate
Big handful of walnuts (40g)
Seeds from ½ vanilla pod or 2 tsp vanilla essence
1 cup plain flour
1 tbsp baking powder
Pinch of salt

Melt the butter in a pan over a lowish heat and then beat in the sugar until well combined. Beat the eggs into the sugar–butter mixture and get the lot as fluffy and light as possible. Now smash the bananas, chocolate and walnuts and stir into the mixture along with the vanilla seeds. Add the flour, baking powder and salt a little at a time, beating together to make sure there are no dry lumps. Now pour the lot into your foil tray. Cover with a large inverted pan above it to reflect the heat from the fire onto the top of the bake (or use a lid on bbq).

Bake for 30 minutes (check that it's not burning after 20). When it's firm to the touch, has gone a bit golden and a knife comes out clean, then it's ready. Allow to cool for 10 minutes off the heat as it continues to bake inside.

Tips

— *Bake in a loaf tin for a traditional banana bread.*
— *Up to you how big you want your banana, chocolate and walnut pieces to be.*
— *Once the cake has cooled, cut into portions, spread butter on each side, and cover with a fine sprinkling of sugar. Then grill the pieces on a metal grill over a gentle fire.*

Homemade Butter

Butter goes very well with bread (doh!) and is used in a fair few of the recipes in this book. Do you know how easy it is to make? Only one ingredient and six simple steps. Warning: the smug factor is off the chart with this one. Say after me, 'Yeh, I made that butter!' Feels good, doesn't it?

There are some rules, however:
1. Keep the cream in the bowl while whisking
2. Don't give up (or use non-dairy cream)
3. Delegate this task to the most energetic people around you (kids are usually quite good for this)

MAKES: *250g (a regular pack of butter)*
TAKES: *10 minutes*
KIT: *large bowl, whisk, A4-sized piece of greaseproof paper*
—

500ml double cream, cold
Pinch of sea salt (optional)

Pour the double cream into the bowl then whisk hard and fast until it separates into liquid and little lumps of butter (use the liquid – uncultured buttermilk – in place of beer for the Beer Bread, see page 68). Then with your bare hands squeeze the butter bits into one big lump. Really push as much of the liquid out as you shape it into a ball. The more liquid that comes out the longer it will keep.

You can keep this unsalted as it is or add a big pinch of flaky sea salt. You can also flavour your butter by working in some herbs or garlic (mmm...). I once lucked out with a truffle that was found by a friend's trained mutt. I shaved it (not the dog) into some butter, sliced the butter into generous disks and for a good long while I had a stash of truffle butter in my freezer to melt over steaks – mega yum!

Roll your butter into a lovely log using the greaseproof paper (like a Christmas cracker) and keep chilled.

Tip

— *Honey butter? Um, yes please! Mix a big spoon of honey into your butter for all you could possibly wish for melting into a slice of your warm bread.*

Wild Baking Shortcuts

Ain't got much time? Ain't got no skills? Try any of these quickie recipes for some naked fire cooking:

Mussels Take a bag with you and just throw individual mussels on hot embers (see page 101). Remove with tongs and add a squeeze of lemon.

Spuds Toss potatoes deep into the fire, cover with embers and leave for an hour. Melted butter + cheese = feast.

Corn on the cob Leave all the leaves on and push under the embers for 15 minutes. Butter, salt, nibble, nibble.

S'mores Toast giant marshmallows until golden, then sandwich between chocolate biscuits. Come on!

Popcorn Put corn in a baggy foil parcel, drop on the fire – you'll hear when it's done (also see double-sieve technique on page 93).

Between every two pine trees there is
a door leading to a new way of life

—

John Muir

**When I was eight, my family moved from above our
bakery in the small English town of Chipping Sodbury
to a farm up on the Cotswold escarpment with views
across to Wales. My brother George and I were thick as
thieves, always looking for adventure.**

The move from a poky garden to a farm (where my Dad and
Grandpa were getting busy with the business of growing
and milling wheat) with its fields and woods meant we ran
riot – building dens, redirecting a fun-run around the farm,
spying on hippies en-route to Stonehenge. Chief among
our activities was making fires. We only had television for
a month every Christmas (rented from Radio Rentals) and
we circled things in the TV guide and binged; oh boy, was
the cold turkey bad. By late January we were back playing
outside after school – whittling a bow and arrow or lighting
a fire is what we did. AND IT'S STILL GOOD NOW.

The first meals I remember cooking for myself were done on a campfire, down in the woods with George. Just us against the world, camo-cream on our faces and the smell of wood smoke on our jumpers. A tin of baked beans, with its hazardously sharp top removed with the dexterous use of my Swiss Army knife, thrown into the hot embers of a campfire, the beans stirred with a bark-stripped twig. Eating them brought us nourishment, a sense of accomplishment and a deep and glowing satisfaction. I can still recall this as a treasured happy place.

A spud wrapped in foil and buried in the fire can be a devilishly good thing for a hungry boy. Will it be burnt on the outside? Most likely yes. Will it be undercooked in the middle? Yes, if you're too impatient (what famished lad isn't?) But the smell, the steam, the sweetness of a hot potato, sprinkled with salt and pepper squirrelled away from aeroplane meals and eaten with a spork (remember them?) was the pinnacle of our campfire culinary accomplishments. Well, if kids can do it unaccompanied, so can you. And if you go down to the woods today, oh sister have I got some recipes for you.

———

Poacher's Breakfast

The campfire breakfast of champions. The breakfast hunger slayer. A dish so unctuous, dark, shiny and irresistible it has been known to instantly banish hangovers of Stag Do proportions. The simple premise is you use up any suitable food from the evening before. (In my case it was some venison from the spit-roast deer that made my brother George's weekend in the woods a proper stag do). If you've got things that need using up, and you imagine it'd go well in the pan, stick it in. Build up a bubbling pan of goodness until it can be resisted no more.

MAKES: *enough for 4*
TAKES: *30 minutes (once the fire is going, longer and slower is better though)*
KIT: *large frying pan, wooden spoon, chopping board*

—

Big knob of butter or glug of oil
2 onions, chopped
Selection of meat, roughly chopped – bacon, black pudding, sausages, assorted offal (kidneys, liver etc.)
1 × 400g tin tomatoes
1 × 400g tin baked beans
Handful of chopped herbs (see Note)

Once your fire is hot and the flames have died down a bit, rake it with a stick to create a deep bed of glowing embers. The bed of embers needs to be near to where you are working and on the outside edge of the fire, so that the pan handle can be easily reached and not get too hot. Get all your ingredients to hand and ready and have something to clean your hands with after handling the raw meat.

Plonk your pan on top of the embers and add the butter or oil and shizzle it around the warming pan. Add the chopped onions followed by whatever meat you are using. Once the onions are golden and the meat has started to crisp, pour over the tins of tomatoes and baked beans, continuing to stir all the time. Once everything has melded together in an irresistible way, add the chopped herbs and serve.

Bread, broken into big bits, toasted over the fire on sticks and slathered in butter is the ideal accompaniment, as is a steaming mug of Cowboy Coffee (see page 141). If your breakfast isn't complete without the addition of eggs, see the next recipe for the perfect partner – poached eggs.

Note
At the right time of year a bunch of wild garlic stirred through this is brilliant. If it's not bright green and newly in leaf, take a bunch of fresh parsley with you, to tear up and stir through.

Poached Eggs and a Cracking Egg Revelation

The best poached eggs are made with really, really fresh eggs. For years I've been flummoxed by poaching, trying all manner of techniques. The revelation came with getting our own hens, meaning we could have eggs literally straight from the ... well, you know.

MAKES: *as many as you like*
TAKES: *8–10 minutes*
KIT: *large pan, slotted spoon, warm bowl*
—

1–2 eggs per person (or get your own egg-laying hen)
Sea salt

Put a big pan (almost full) of water on to boil and add some salt. Once it's boiling, reduce the heat to a good simmer by moving to the edge of the fire.

Crack a couple of fresh eggs straight into the water and observe their progress. I don't create a whirlpool. Sometimes I add vinegar for flavour. After a couple of minutes I lift one out on the slotted spoon and give it a tweak. You'll know how you like them and when they are ready (I like mine Instagram-soft in the middle).

Collect them up in a warm bowl and keep warm until you are ready to eat, seasoned with a pinch of sea salt.

Spuds and Bangers

Aka sausage on a stick with a baked potato. This recipe, if you can call it that, is campfire simplicity itself. Top with grated cheese and serve with beans or ratatouille. I like this with a leafy salad and a big glass of red wine. De-flipin'-licious.

MAKES: *as many as you like*
TAKES: *about 1 hour of very light work*
FIRE: *glowing embers*
KIT: *cooking sticks or skewers, small shovel or trowel or strong poky stick, tin foil optional*

—

1 large baking potato per person
2 good-quality sausages per person
Butter and grated cheese, to serve (optional)
Salt and pepper

Once your fire has died down to glowing embers, rake them to one side from the centre and make a hollow space. Lower in your potatoes and cover them first with ash then with the hot embers. I leave my spuds for an hour to bake. Literally *pomme de terre*!

Meanwhile take your fancy gourmet sausage of choice and run it through lengthways with your sharpened stick. I like to use a long stick as my cooking method is to place a brick-sized stone next to the fire then drive the non-sausage end of the stick into the ground. I can then ingeniously pivot my sausage above the glowing embers. The stone acts as a heat reflector as I twizzle my stick, slowly rotating the sausage, rotisserie-style, until cooked to perfection.

You will know when your potatoes are cooked when a knife can be easily pushed into the centre. With a little practice, your jacket potatoes and sausages will both be ready at the same time.

Tips

— *You can of course wrap your potatoes in foil first. My favourite way is to slather the spud with olive oil and a generous sprinkling of flaky sea salt.*

— *If you're nervous about your sausages being cooked properly, they are especially girthful, or you have lots to do, it's not a bad idea to boil your sausages in water first, then simply finish them off over the fire for a lovely crispy skin.*

— *For the ultimate wild hot dog: combine your sausage on a stick with Snobrød (see page 64) that has been twisted around a stick of sausage thickness. When the sausage is cooked and the bread is baked, with a little lubrication (think Dijon mustard, ketchup, hot sauce) you can slide your sausage the length of the doughy pockets of joy, before sitting back and enjoying the reward for your efforts around a warm campfire with a large glass of wine.*

— *If you keep the potato skins, you can fry them up the next day to make awesome chips.*

Two-sieve Popcorn

Fancy a wee DIY project? This is super-easy and hugely rewarding and is a wonderful thing to do with kids of all ages. By hinging two sieves together with a little wire and attaching the sieves to a stick, you can make a closed basket for your corn, that can be safely held over the fire. Then you get to watch the corn popping right in front of your eyes.

MAKES: *as much you like*
TAKES: *30 minutes to construct*
KIT: *2 matching metal sieves, 1 metre of firm but pliable wire, pliers (if you have a Leatherman, now is the time to use it), a decent stick – half the length and a similar width to a broom handle*

—

Popping corn
Salt or sugar, to taste

Using the wire and pliers, hinge the two sieves together at the opposite end to the handles, so they form a neat-fitting cylinder when closed. Now, fix the sieves so the bottom one is bound to the stick and the top sieve closes down on top. You might need to bend the sieve handles to achieve a good fit between the metal sieve rims so the popcorn doesn't escape. Finally make a wire ring to hold the top sieve closed during the popping. A groove cut into the top part of the stick can also help to hold the sieve baskets in place.

Once everything is secure, add a handful of corn into the bottom sieve basket. Close the top and secure. Hold the cornpoption over your fire. It's wildly good to see your corn popping over the fire, so quickly and willingly. Wait for the sieve metal to cool down for a minute before carefully opening. Add salt or sugar to taste. Repeat.

Spit-roast Stag with Whisky and Beer

This isn't a recipe, more the sharing of an idea. Several years ago my brother George got married and I was his best man. As best man it was my duty to arrange the stag do, to which he had invited 20 or so guys – good friends of his from school, university, army officer training, church and the various places he's worked. Most people didn't know each other, but after speaking to them I realised my biggest challenge was overcoming 'stag do exhaustion'. After a long season of stag dos in Dublin, Prague and Ibiza, many of the guys were nearly ruined in more ways than one. My remedy was to host something simple in the woods.

I ordered a whole gutted deer from our local butcher and invited everyone to come in old clothes and bring some whisky and I bought a barrel of beer from the local brewery. Between us we had enough skills to dig a fire pit, build a spit, skin a deer and eat it before everyone got too famished. I bought some dough from the bakery with me in a bucket with a lid on, and we baked flattish breads on a shovel placed over the fire.

I called in a few favours and we were treated to massages (all above board) and beguiling belly dancing. Some weird shit went down that I can't tell you about, starting with an uphill-downhill tug-of-war ... The whole lot came in at £28 per head. Some powerful bonding happened around that fire, which we happily reminisce about even now. That's the kind of stag do we do, and I commend it to you, in the spirit of wild baking.

Spruce Tip Tea

As an antidote to all that stag do revelry, this is a refreshing, mild-flavoured tea, rich in vitamins C and A. The soothing drink has a medicinal quality that can stave off scurvy if you're in the woods for an exceedingly long time. More regularly it's used for keeping a cold at bay.

Gather a handful of needles from the very ends of the branches of a spruce pine tree – you want the brightest, greenest needles on the tree. Trim the woody ends off, tear or chop the needles and put into a pot. You want about a handful of needles per cup of tea. Pour over just-boiled water and leave it to steep for 5 minutes or so. Strain through a cloth or an old clean sock and enjoy. To sweeten, add a spoon of honey or maple syrup. More tea, Vicar?

Caution

Make sure you research your spruces before you make this. There are three pine trees that are poisonous to use – Yew, Norfolk Island Pine and Ponderosa Pine – so please check first to see you don't do yourself a mischief. DO NOT make tea with yew tree needles as these are very toxic.

Spruce tip tea is powerful stuff not recommended for those that are pregnant.

4
Beach

No, I saw the sea first!

—

Anyone

Wild baking on a beach is a powerful and life-enhancing experience. There's the sound of the waves, the enlivening smell of ozone and on a good day, the bright light reflected off the sea to warm your cockles.

Any trip to the sea can become an adventure when you take some matches and good food to cook. Just over 20 years ago, not long after I bought a little Peugeot with money from doing shifts in the bakery, I took a young lady, her friend and my sister to Branscombe on the south coast of Devon. It was my first day off and one of those glorious early summer days. At the beach I found a rowing boat that we could hire for only a few quid.

We took it out and sploshed about before noticing a reel of fishing wire in the bottom of the boat with a couple of hooks. We were in luck: flickers of silver passed under the boat. With nothing to use as bait, I nonetheless lowered the hooks and in no time at all caught two glistening mackerel.

Back on the beach I gutted them with my Swiss Army knife. In the back of my car I had a disposable barbecue for just such an opportunity as this. They were grilled simply and we devoured them, just as they were, fresh from the sea.

I can remember that day – the mix tape we played in the car, the feeling of speed, driving with the windows down, the flavours of the fish – just as if it happened yesterday. And the young lady, Anna, and I have now been married for 18 wonderful years. Powerful things happen when you bake on the beach. So be careful, you might catch more than fish.

10TH ANNIVERSARY

Mussels Baked in Embers

I love mussels. They're the most carbon-positive form of protein. I've tried them every which way, and for me, hands down, this is the best. Seafood doesn't get simpler than this.

MAKES: *enough for 2*
TAKES: *5 minutes*
FIRE: *embers*
KIT: *metal tongs*

—

4 big handfuls of mussels, scrubbed
1 lemon
Chilled bottle of white wine

Once your campfire has burnt down to its embers, push a handful of mussels, one at a time, hinge side down, halfway into the embers. Within a minute or two the mussels will open and steam cook themselves with the sea brine within, and their own delicious juices. Deftly whip them out using your tongs, add a squeeze of lemon and eat them directly from the fire. Just accompany with chilled white wine.
Bon appetit!

Tips
— *Long metal tongs will help prevent you from getting burnt. It is harder though to get them in and out of the embers without losing precious juices.*
— *If a mussel stays open after you've given it a knock (before baking), then it was already dead and too risky to eat. Throw these ones back into the sea.*
— *If you bake the mussels for too long they become chewy and hard. Not long enough, and they'll be slimy and cold. With a bit of practice you'll get it just right.*

Grilled Mackerel with Burnt Lemon

Mackerel is best enjoyed fresh. As you can see from my introductory anecdote, it is simplicity itself to cook, giving you more time to enjoy the beach and sea.

MAKES: *enough for 2*
TAKES: *5–10 minutes*
FIRE: *grill*
KIT: *sharp knife*

—

4 whole mackerel
1 lemon
Sea salt

Catch your mackerel or buy them fresh, light a campfire and make ready a grill.

To gut your mackerel, you'll need a sharp knife. Hold them with the back in the palm of your hand and make an incision where you imagine the throat to be (opposite the spine). Run your knife down the length of the body to the poop hole. This will expose all the innards. Using your finger, whip them out, and if necessary trim any dangly bits inside with your knife. It's a messy job but really very easy. (Although if you're buying them from a fishmonger, I would ask them to do this for you.) Discard the innards (sparing a thought for nature) and give your mackerel a rinse in the sea. Super-fresh mackerel can tend to curl up on the grill, so give each fillet (side) three slashes to the bone.

Slice your lemon into fat discs and char them on both sides. Then season the mackerel with a pinch of sea salt and cook on your hot grill (see page 39). If the grill is not hot enough the skin can end up sticking to it. Mackerel cooks very quickly – you only need a couple of minutes on each side. Serve the mackerel with the charred lemon to squeeze over the oily fish.

Poached Salmon Tartine

If you fancy pushing the boat out and making something truly spectacular, this one's for you. Get it right, and you'll enjoy fancy restaurant-standard cuisine, cooked in a cool box.

MAKES: *enough for 2*
TAKES: *1 hour*
KIT: *clean and empty cool box, big bucket full of cold seawater, large pan, thermometer, ziplock bag, sharp knife, chopping board, small bowl, toasting fork or suitable stick*

—

2 eggs
2 × 250g salmon fillets
4 tbsp rapeseed oil
1 shallot, finely chopped
4 anchovy fillets, roughly chopped
1 glug of red wine vinegar
2 big slices of sourdough bread (see page 53)
1 baby lettuce, shredded
8 ripe cherry tomatoes, chopped
6 big caperberry stalks
Salt and pepper

Once your fire has died down enough to heat your pan, boil up a couple of litres of water and pour into a small cooler box. Gently lower your eggs into the hot water to cook for 11 minutes, then transfer them to the bucket of seawater to cool. Meanwhile put another litre of water above the fire to boil.

Slowly add cold water from the bucket to the hot water in the cool box until it reads 55°c on your thermometer.

Season the salmon and place into the ziplock bag with a tablespoon of oil.

Lower the salmon into the water, allowing the air to escape as you lower it in. Seal the bag at the last moment, with a minimal amount of air inside, and drop it into the water. Place the lid on top of the cool box and leave the salmon to poach for 12 minutes, checking the temperature often and adding a little hot water to adjust the temperature when it drops below 55°C.

Next up, put the shallot and anchovies into a small bowl with the vinegar and the remaining oil and mash it all together with a fork. Toast your sourdough bread over the fire.

When the 12 minutes are up, remove your beautifully poached salmon from the bag, break up into chunks, leaving the skin behind, and serve on top of toasted bread with the lettuce and tomatoes.

Remove the eggs from their shells, cut them in half and place on top. Add the caperberries, season to taste and drizzle over the anchovy dressing. Serve immediately.

Surf 'n' Turf: Lamb Koftas and Lobster

Lamb koftas and succulent lobster cooked on a grill on the beach, eaten as the sun goes down. Served with a garlicky brandy butter and a heavenly fattoush salad, it's perfect with a side of Ash-baked Sourdough Flatbreads (see page 57). This recipe holds a fond place in the Herbert family food book. Personally I prefer to prep this in the kitchen and then invite people in the party to all carry a contribution to the beach fire. It's a long recipe but deceptively easy to make. This is a full-on celebration recipe and would be ideal for an alternative or tropical Christmas.

MAKES: *enough for 12*
TAKES: *2 hours*
FIRE: *a decent bed of embers set up for a grill*
KIT: *2 chopping boards, metal tongs, 2 bowls, 12 metal skewers, fridge or cool box, spoons, small pan, baking tray, clean jar with lid, wheelbarrow (or similar) to carry everything to your chosen wild beach destination*
—

For the kebabs
1.8kg lamb (or venison) mince
2 red onions, finely chopped
3 red chillies, finely diced
6 garlic cloves, crushed
1½ tsp crushed chilli flakes
1 tbsp ground coriander
1 tbsp ground cumin
1 tsp ground juniper berries
5 tbsp roughly chopped coriander leaves
Juice of 1 large lemon
500g Greek yoghurt (1 big pot)
3 tbsp finely chopped mint leaves
Salt and pepper

For the lobster

6 cooked lobsters, halved lengthways
400g salted butter
6 garlic cloves, crushed
4 tbsp roughly chopped parsley
Squeeze of lemon juice
100ml brandy

For the fattoush

4 big slices of sourdough, diced into croutonish cubes
2 tbsp olive oil
750g baby plum tomatoes, halved lengthways
1 large cucumber, thickly sliced
3 red onions, thinly sliced
2 large handfuls of mint leaves, picked
2 large handfuls of parsley leaves, picked
3 tbsp red wine vinegar
6 tbsp extra-virgin olive oil
1 tbsp sumac

Put the lamb mince into a bowl with the onion, chillies, 4 of the garlic cloves, spices, coriander and lemon juice and mix well, squeezing all the ingredients together. Season generously and mix once more.

Divide into 12 balls then press around 12 metal skewers, forming long sausages. If you have time, put in the fridge to set for 30 minutes.

Place your grill rack above a very hot part of the fire, above non-flaming embers (if you are doing this at home, heat a griddle pan or your barbecue until smoking hot). Add the skewers and cook the kebabs, rotating 90° every 1–2 minutes, until browned on all sides and just cooked through.

Meanwhile, mix the yoghurt, mint and remaining crushed garlic together then season with salt and pepper to taste.

Place the lobster, cut side down, onto the hot grill rack/barbecue/griddle pan. Cook for 2–3 minutes until charred, then flip and cook for another 2 minutes on the shell side until hot through.

Heat the butter and garlic in a pan until the butter has melted and the garlic just lightly cooked. Add the parsley, a squeeze of lemon juice and the brandy and season with salt and pepper. Don't be tempted to flambé as it makes the butter very bitter!

Now for the fattoush. Prepare a place just above the fire to toast the sourdough. Scatter the sourdough bits onto a baking tray and drizzle with the olive oil and salt and pepper. Toast until just golden and crispy, then remove and leave to cool.

Put the tomatoes, cucumber, red onion, mint and parsley into a bowl and toss together. In a jar shake together the vinegar, extra-virgin olive oil and sumac, then drizzle over the salad. Add the croutons and toss the whole lot together.

Serve the kebabs with a dollop of mint yoghurt, the lobster alongside with a generous drizzle of brandy butter and a pile of salad to finish it off.

Vegetarian 'I Can't Believe There's No Meat, This Is Amazing!' Chilli 🏠 ✳

When we go on a family camping trip, more often than not, we'll make a big chilli the day before, take it with us on the journey, and heat it up as we're setting up camp. The great thing about veggie chilli is that it's all low-risk foods (no meat), and most people can eat it. It's a relatively cheap and calorific meal for the hungry ones, and on a cooler night, this raises the bar in terms of comfort food. Also the non-perishable nature of the ingredients makes this chilli an ideal end-of-trip meal, as the ingredients don't need to be kept cool. Warning: contains beans. Lash those wind flaps.

MAKES: *enough for 6*
TAKES: *30 minutes' prep, plus a couple of hours' slow cooking (but longer is better)*
FIRE: *low and slow friendly fire*
KIT: *chopping board, sharp knife, sieve, Dutch oven or large heavy pan with a lid, metal tongs, wooden spoon, large bowl, a tripod for hanging your pot above the fire would be ideal*

—

1 cup spelt or barley grains
1 cup lentils (any type)
Generous glug of oil
1 cinnamon stick
1 tbsp cumin seeds
1 tbsp coriander seeds
4 onions (2 red, 2 white is good), chopped
½ head of garlic, cloves smashed
3 red peppers (check out charring option on page 112 for extra flavour), deseeded and roughly chopped
1 green pepper, deseeded and roughly chopped
2 × 400g tins chopped tomatoes

1 × 400g tin kidney beans, drained and sieve-rinsed
2 whole Scotch bonnet chillies (or similar)
1 cup strong black coffee (see page 141)
Big squeeze of tomato purée
3 tbsp muscovado sugar
½ bar dark chocolate (I would say a whole bar, but
**   I usually end up eating half)**
Salt and pepper
Big handful of fresh coriander
Soured cream, to serve

Soak your grains and lentils in 2 cups of water – the longer the better. Meanwhile, set your Dutch oven up over a low-medium heat and add the oil and whole spices. Add the chopped onions and, once they are golden, add the smashed garlic. Add the peppers and allow to soften for 5 minutes, stirring occasionally to see nothing burns to the bottom (add a dash more oil if things are sticking).

Now add the tinned tomatoes and drained and rinsed beans. Swill the tomato tins out with water and add this to the chilli too. Add all the remaining ingredients (except the coriander), including the grains and lentils and their starchy water. Stir the whole lot together and pop the lid on.

Drink any spare coffee (cook's bonus). Stir the chilli occasionally, checking for seasoning and chilli heat and making sure it doesn't catch on the bottom (top up with more water if needed). After about 1 hour, your chilli should be lovely and thick – once the grains are soft with a little bite, the chilli is done. You know how you like your chilli.

Stir in the chopped coriander and serve with a big dollop of soured cream. It's also ace with a smashed avocado and goes really well with the Cornbread (see page 71) and baked potatoes (see page 89).

Tips

— Add the Scotch bonnet chilies to the pot whole. Periodically taste your chilli – when the heat level is just right you can whip these out.

— For a lovely extra depth of sweet smoky flavour, grill your peppers first directly on the embers, turning them occasionally with metal tongs. Once the skin is charred and black all over, allow them to cool in a large bowl covered with clingfilm. After 5–10 minutes, the charred skins will easily slip off. Deseed and proceed.

— A favourite in our house is cheapie tortilla wraps, cut into big triangles, and fried in some oil until crispy. These are then used as a tasty spade to shovel the chilli into your cake hole. Spud skins are also ideal.

— Make this at home, freeze and take it with you frozen. It'll keep your other perishable ingredients cool as it defrosts.

— This pot gets better with time, so if you want to make the most of spending time with the people you're with, make this the day before. And come hungry o'clock, simply heat and serve. Faff-free wild cooking.

Your mountain is waiting so get on your way

—

Dr. Seuss

A trip into the mountains, if you plan it right, is a great investment in your wellbeing, forcing clean air into your lungs. When the sky is clear and the views are majestic, a trip into the mountains can give you a fresh perspective on life. The recipes in this chapter will help fuel your ascent, be a treat for when you make it to the top or provide you with something warm and rewarding on your return. Most importantly, they tip the hat at lightweight ingredients and kit, for cooking on the hoof.

A couple of years ago I bought a jet boil stove for my son Milo. This little rocket is no bigger than a Thermos flask and transforms from inside itself into a water boiler extraordinaire. Not long after, Milo and I took the stove for a mini adventure in the Brecon Beacons in Wales. En-route we called into an outdoor adventure store and stocked up on food that only required boiled water. Needless to say it was a mixed bag. The highlights included single-estate fair-trade coffee in an airtight pouch that you pour nearly boiling water into, and after a few minutes, pour it into your mug; and variations on a posh Pot Noodle, very light and not too bad. The most ingenious was a Full English Breakfast in a pouch. You snap something inside (but separate from the food) that creates a chemical reaction to warm it up. It heats the food so it's piping hot in a matter of minutes. It wasn't the best Full English, but just the reward we needed at the top of the snowy Pen Y Fan. A remarkable innovation, leaving much space for us to make and enjoy real food.

———

The Energy Bar 🏠
(aka Uncle Marcus's Flapjack)

Energy bars, energy bars, energy bars! Come on people, they're easy to make, smell amazing when cooking, and will fuel you up a mountain.

Recently I joined my uncle Marcus for a few days' baking at RCK (Refugee Community Kitchen), an extraordinary organisation run by volunteers, making (at the time I went) 3,000 delicious and nutritious hot meals a day using entirely donated food, or food bought with money that's been raised. I saw from their Facebook posts that oats were needed. So I collected 100kg from a wholesaler in Bristol and loaded them into my car. Over the next three days, using this exact recipe, I was able to make 32 trays of delicious and filling flapjacks to hand out locally.

One of the brilliant things about this recipe is all the delicious and energy-boosting ingredients you can add to it. I've made it with melted dark chocolate, small cubes of stem ginger, handfuls of mixed seeds, but you could use any combination of dried fruit and/or nuts. In the RCK warehouse I found a big pack of salted caramel popcorn, so I pushed popcorn into the top of the warm flapjack mixture, just before baking. And – true story alert – they were not long out of the oven before they caught the eye of Pamela Anderson who happened to be visiting. Bucket list, tick! It is said this combination has magic powers. Basically go wild, get energy!

As an aside, whoever you are, if you can spare a few days, especially if you're a trainee cook or wannabe chef, doing a stage with RCK or a similar organisation will give you a fantastic insight into catering for thousands of people at one service, to a very high standard. It'll be fantastic on your CV, you'll have a blast while supporting a good cause, and likely meet some great people and make good friends to boot.

MAKES: *12 bars*
TAKES: *45 minutes*
KIT: *small pan, wooden spoon, dough scraper, small roasting tin or foil tray*

—

250g (1 pack) butter, plus extra for greasing the pan
5 tbsp sugar
5 tbsp golden syrup
3½ cups oats
Optional extras: chopped dark chocolate, nuts, seeds, dried fruit, popcorn

Measure the butter, sugar and golden syrup into a small pan and heat together until the sugar has dissolved and the butter has melted. Measure out the oats into a mixing bowl and add anything yummy that takes your fancy. Dried apple and toasted cobnuts with a pinch of cinnamon anyone?

Pour the melted sweet butter mix over the oats and stir together until there are no dry bits. Rub the inside of your tray with a little butter to stop the mixture from sticking.

Dollop the mixture into the tray and using a dough scraper smoooooth it down and work it into the corners.

Bake at 170°c for 20 minutes or until it starts to go golden at the edges. Once done, leave to cool for a couple of minutes then mark out the slices or pieces you desire using your dough scraper and push right through the mixture (you'll find it much harder to do this once the flapjack has set hard).

Golden Eagle Scrambled Eggs

Make this as golden as possible by using organic eggs; they tend to have darker, richer yolks.

Break a couple of eggs carefully into a pan – don't let the yolks break until the last moment. When the eggs are nearly cooked, take the pan off the heat, add a big knob of butter and finally break the yolks, stirring the lot together, until it's golden silky and smooth. Season and serve.

Cheddar Craft Beer Fondue

Throughout my life I've been lucky enough to spend the occasional week skiing in the Alps. All that activity makes you hungry, and with all that lush pasture buried under the snow, it's only natural we should consume vast quantities of melted cheese (the pasture feeds the animals that make the milk that becomes the cheese). Raclette is a favourite, but for sheer cheesiness and love of sharing, it has to be fondue.

Choose an IPA or similar craft beer, as long as it's not bitter, stout or anything too dark or strong in flavour. Finding a locally brewed beer and a strong local cheese (that's good for melting) is a great opportunity to discover even more of what the area has to offer.

MAKES: *enough for 4*
TAKES: *1 hour*
KIT: *large pan, cheese grater, large bowl, skewers (or pointy sticks), whisk*

—

400ml beer (open two 330ml bottles and drink most of one while you cook)
1kg mature Cheddar, coarsely grated
1½ tbsp cornflour
1 tsp English mustard powder
Salami, cooked sausage, pickles and hunks of sourdough, for dipping

Place the beer in a large pan, bring to a simmer and reduce by half.

Meanwhile, mix the cornflour and mustard powder through the grated cheese so it has an even coating. Add the cheese to the reduced beer a handful at a time, whisking continuously until it is smooth and creamy. *Et voilà!* Obviously, it would be daft not to match the beer in the fondue and drink more of the same.

Burgoo Stew with Bourbon and Hot Sauce

This is a one-pot wonder from Kentucky. Since before the Civil War, it has been made in massive kettles for big gatherings like Derby Day. This is more of a dish to make at the bottom of the mountain (or at home) to reheat once you're up the mountain. It's an empty-the-fridge kind of dish that has to be made with at least three types of meat. I like mine cooked into a delicious, brown, undifferentiated mess that you can stand the wooden spoon in. Like most stews it's even better the next day.

Follow The Burgoo Rules:
1. Make with at least three types of meat
2. Cook for a minimum of 6 hours
3. Cook outdoors over an open fire

MAKES: *enough for 16*
TAKES: *6 hours*
KIT: *large heavy-based pan, big plate, tongs*

—

Oil
1kg cheap and tasty stewing beef, cut into big cubes
1kg pork – belly or something tasty, cut into big cubes
1 large chicken, jointed or cut into several large pieces
6 large onions, chopped
Bunch of carrots, scrubbed and sliced
Bunch of celery, chopped
Big handful of okra, slit lengthways (or 2 green peppers, deseeded and sliced)
4 red peppers, deseeded and sliced
1.5 litres beef or chicken stock
2 × 400g tins chopped tomatoes
1 whole tube of tomato purée
1 × 400g tin butter beans, drained
Glug of Worcestershire sauce

Shake of Tabasco
4 corn on the cob, quartered lengthways
1 cup bourbon
Bunch of parsley, leaves torn
Soured cream and Cornbread (see page 71), to serve

Heat a large pan with a glug of oil, add the meat in batches and sear all sides, getting a good caramelisation (mmm...). Transfer the meat to a plate.

Add a glug more oil to the pan, add the onions and cook until softened. Add the carrots and celery, then the okra (or green peppers) and red peppers. Once this has all softened up nicely, pour over the stock and add the chopped tomatoes, tomato purée, butter beans, Worcestershire sauce and a fierce shake of Tabasco.

Right, in with that lovely caramelised meat. Leave to simmer over a low heat for at least 6 hours, stirring occasionally and adding water as required.

Half an hour before you want to eat, add the quartered corn cobs and continue to simmer.

Taste and adjust the seasoning with any combination of salt, pepper, Worcestershire sauce or Tabasco. Add the bourbon and stir through the parsley.

Once your stew has achieved the desired consistency and the flavour is on point, serve in bowls with a dollop of soured cream, a side of cornbread and, of course, another cup of bourbon. Who's ready for a hoedown?

Chorizo Tatties 🏠

I recently met mountain man Alec Farmer, founder of Trakke bags, for supper at The Dogs in Edinburgh. The conversation strolled into Wild Baking territory; his 'go to' ingredient is chorizo. Hot and delicious, the cooked variety (so low risk) will produce enough fat to oil a sizzling pan and is good at any time of day. His other tip is to always have a hard-boiled egg or two on you. Packed by nature in biodegradable packaging it's always ready to go with just a pinch of salt.

So Alec, this one's for you. Chorizo and eggs, both in the same bowl, with potatoes for necessary carbs.

MAKES: *enough for 2*
TAKES: *30 minutes*
KIT: *pan, chopping board, knife*

—

2 big handfuls of small salad potatoes
4 eggs
1 length of chorizo, sliced
1 onion, diced
Bunch of parsley, leaves torn
Salt and pepper
2 litres of water

Chop up any potatoes larger than an egg yolk to reduce the cooking time. Put into a pan of water, add a big pinch of salt and put over the heat to boil.

Once it comes to the boil, add your still-in-their-shell eggs and set the timer on your phone for 7 minutes for a soft centre. When the time is up whip them out, and allow to cool a bit. Continue boiling the potatoes for a further 10 minutes or until they are soft when you push a knife into them.

Meanwhile, slice your chorizo and dice your onion. Drain the potatoes and set aside on a plate or bowl. Return the pan to the heat, add the chorizo and fry; if it's a fat one, it'll yield some of its spicy fat. Once the slices have started to go a bit crispy, lower the temperature and add the onion.

After 5 minutes the onion will have softened so add the li'l potatoes back in and stir. I like it if the potatoes smash a little bit; if you only stir occasionally some of the potatoes' skins will go a bit crispy, which I love too.

Right, enough of that nonsense, it's smelling so good, this is some kinda olfactorious torture. Stir through the parsley along with a pinch of salt and some pepper and tip into a bowl. Peel the eggs, cut each in half and place them on top of the potatoes. Season again (you must have a bit of salt on each egg). Dive in.

Tip
— *If it's the right season for wild garlic and you pass some on your way, grab a big handful, rinse and use instead of parsley.*

Basecamp Burgers

Once you've tried burgers, slider style, you won't go back.
Try to make the effort to source well-hung, dry-aged mince.
Chuck steak is perfect and a bit of fat is good in the mince too.
It will be naturally sticky and bind together like a beaut.

MAKES: *4 burgers*
TAKES: *15 minutes*
FIRE: *hot fire, grill*
KIT: *frying pan, burger flipper, knife and chopping board*

—

400g chuck steak mince
2 tbsp oil
1 onion, very thinly sliced
4 slices of burger cheese (as dirty or tasteful as you like)
4 decent burger baps
Salt and pepper

Divide the mince into 4 equal balls and roll them round.

Heat the oil in a frying pan on a grill over your fire and when
it's smoking hot add the balls of mince. Season with salt and
pepper and allow to brown for 1 minute, then push a pinch of
sliced onions into the middle and 'slam' the burger flat with
the burger flipper.

Flip the burger over so the onions can brown off and melt into
the meat. Cook for a further 2 minutes, or longer if you don't
like pink meat. Place a piece of cheese on top of each burger
then place the top half of the bap on top of the burger, and sit
the bottom half on top of the lot. This way the cheese melts
to the bread and the bap warms through.

Cook for a minute or two more then slide the lot off the
grill and flip the bottom of the bap under the burger.
Chin-drippingly delicious.

If there is magic on this planet, it is contained in water

—

Lauren Eisley

Time on the river never seems wasted. Messing around on boats, just going with the flow, the sound of water gently lapping the side of your canoe, dappled sunlight through the trees on the bank. The exhilaration and terror of the rapids, and the getting back to where you started: it's all hungry work. So here are some recipes to keep you fed.

One of my favourite epicurious river trips was a stolen Monday in March with my mate Marc. We needed some time out and fancied fishing, so we borrowed rods and kit, secured one-day fishing licences and headed to a remote river.

We packed a little barbecue, a lovely sourdough loaf, a really nice bottle of white wine to keep chilled in the river, a lemon and salt and pepper. As we set off, it occurred to me (well, my stomach) that if we don't catch anything, it would be a lousy lunch. So we swung by our local fishmonger who, because it was Monday, only had mackerel.

Well, we did catch some trout, but it was while the mackerel was on the barbecue that some old boys, with their fishing kit and tackle, slowed down as they walked by. First they admired our sophisticated-looking lunch set-up, then were utterly perplexed as to how we had found mackerel so far up the river. How we laughed. And it must've been tiring, because as the sun came out and warmed our grassy bank, with our bellies full of loaves, fishes and wine, we both had a little snooze. By the time I woke up, things had gone a bit Brokeback Mountain (to the casual observer anyway) as Marc's nose was in my armpit. Happy days!

Hot Stone Bacon Bap with Smashed Tom Relish and a One-egg Omelette

Who doesn't love a bacon bap to start a day of wild adventuring? The smell alone can coax a bear outta hibernation. The addition of a tart, sticky relish cuts through any fat and if you like your relish hot, just add a diced chilli and a bit more paprika. To stack it higher, both with calories and vertically, add in a one-egg omelette, or make it veggie perfect by leaving out the bacon. Go vegan with a smoky aubergine slice (see page 134).

Jamie Oliver made a one-egg omelette for me last summer at an outdoor breakfast and it's featured in all our wild breakfasts since. They are killer good and are perfect in a breakfast bap because unlike a fried egg, you've no mess from 'lancing the yolk'.

MAKES: *4 breakfast baps*
TAKES: *20 minutes*
KIT: *hot oiled stone/grill/frying pan, wooden spoon, fork, palette knife/burger flipper, cup*

—

8 rashers of dry-cured bacon
4 rolls

For the relish
Big pinch of fennel seeds
1 tbsp smoked paprika
Glug of oil
1 onion, chopped
1 × 400g tin chopped tomatoes
1 tbsp sugar (or use honey or black treacle)
Pinch of salt and pepper
Handful of fresh herbs (parsley is traditional, oregano or basil takes it to the Med)
½ lemon

For the one-egg omelette (per person)
Knob of butter
1 egg
Handful of grated Cheddar
Salt and pepper

Set up a hot stone or grill you can cook on while you make the relish. Add the fennel seeds to a small pan and toast for a couple of minutes, then add the paprika and oil. After a minute add the onion and when it starts to soften and go golden add the tomatoes, sugar and seasoning. Continue to cook over a gentle heat for about 10 minutes until the relish has reduced to a yummy stickiness. Stir in the herbs and a squeeze of lemon. Allow to cool a bit and you're good to go. As well as being perfect in a bacon bap, this is great with a bit of cheese or some cold meat.

Grill the bacon while you make the omelettes.

Heat a frying pan while you fork up an egg in a cup and season with salt and pepper. Focus now as you have to work fast. Add a knob of butter to the hot pan and sizzle it around. Pour the egg into the centre and add a small handful of Cheddar on top. Quickly fold the edges over the cheese using your flat metal implement of choice. Flip it over and give it maximum 30 seconds on the other side – the trick is to get them soft and melty-cheesy. And when you've everything to hand it's quite easy to make one a minute, which is handy if you've lots of people to feed.

Smoky Aubergine Slice

Slice your aubergine (eggplant for those in the US) to your preferred thickness (little-finger-width is good) and rub with olive oil. Season with salt and pepper and a pinch of smoky paprika. Grill for a couple of minutes on both sides over a good heat. Smoked salt or some damp/soaked wood chips added to the fire will give your aubergine a smokier flavour.

Can't Cook, Won't Bake Baba Ganoush

If you never cook and only ever burn things, this is the dish for you. All you've got to lose is 15 minutes of your life and what you risk is changing the perception of yourself with a delicious dish that's perfect as a dip.

MAKES: *2 servings*
TAKES: *30 minutes*
FIRE: *hot*
KIT: *sharp stick, sharp knife, chopping board*

—

1 aubergine
1 red chilli, chopped
2 garlic cloves, chopped
Fresh parsley, chopped
Juice of ½ lemon
Olive oil
Salt and pepper

Make a fork out of wood, like a catapult with sharp prongs and a very long handle. Fix an aubergine to the fork and hold it over a hot fire until it's burnt on all sides. If your stick looks like it might burn you can wrap it with foil. The aubergine will shrink and go squishy after about 15 minutes. Let it cool.

Put the chopped chilli, garlic, parsley, lemon juice and oil in a bowl and season with salt and pepper. Using a tablespoon, scoop out the soft smoky flesh of the aubergine, chop up and stir into the bowl. Taste for seasoning, pat yourself on the back and give yourself a secret smile.

How to Hot Smoke Fish

Credit for this natty set-up goes to my brother and partner-in-crime Henry. He first did this at home one Christmas while he was still at catering college. Salmon was smoked under a wooden box that was ceremoniously lifted, wafting the smoke, like dry ice, in the middle of the table. We've since recreated this delicious and dramatic feat at many food festivals.

MAKES: *as many smoked fillets as you like*
TAKES: *about 15 minutes*
FIRE: *setup for grill and hot embers*
KIT: *large frying pan, large metal mixing bowl, oven gloves or towel, stainless steel (not plastic-coated) wire cooling rack, foil*
—

Handful of dry rice
2 tbsp sugar
1 aromatic herbal tea bag (jasmine, chamomile, fennel)
1 salmon fillet per person, mackerel and trout also work well

Place a sheet of foil in the frying pan. Add the rice and sugar and the contents of the tea bag and put the pan over the heat.

Place the cooling wire on the pan above the rice mix, Once the aromatic mix starts to smoke, place the fish on the wire cooling rack and the inverted bowl over the fish to trap the smoke inside. After about 8 minutes, the fish will have taken on an attractive tanning-salon hue.

Because it is hot as well as smoky under the bowl, the fish will be both smoked and cooked. Use a knife to check the fish is done just as you'd like. Ideally it'll be somewhere between sashimi raw and hard-done-by. Once the rice mix has cooled a bit, scrunch up the foil and dispose of carefully. Bonus: no washing up! Burnt sugar mix is *not* desireable especially when you're wild baking.

Hot smoked salmon is divine on a slice of Beer Bread (see page 68) with some horseradish sauce.

Smoked Salmon

Whether it's Christmas morning, a wedding breakfast or
a special day in the great outdoors, this recipe punches
well above its weight for flavour, drama and general
impressiveness relative to the modest effort required to make
it. And yes, it's much better than cold shop-bought smoked
salmon. If you caught the salmon yourself, why wouldn't you
honour the catch in this deliciously ceremonious way.

MAKES: *enough for 2*
TAKES: *2 hours tops*
KIT: *grill, 2 foil trays, bowl, dish*

—

½ cup caster sugar, plus 1 tbsp for the mini smoker
½ cup flaky sea salt
2 tbsp pink peppercorns, lightly crushed
¼ cup gin
2 × 200g skin-on salmon fillets, pin-boned
500g rice
1 aromatic tea bag (chamomile is great)

Mix the sugar, salt and peppercorns together in a bowl until
well mixed then add the gin and stir to make a paste. Spread
one-third of the paste over the bottom of a dish.

Lay the salmon fillets on top, skin side down, then spread the
rest of the salt paste over the top of the salmon to cover totally.

Place somewhere cool for as long as you can (ideally an hour
or overnight somewhere cool, 0–8°C). Knock or brush the
paste off the salmon then pat the salmon dry. Now follow the
method on previous page.

Tip
— *If you leave this in a fridge tightly wrapped in clingfilm for*
3 days, pouring out the liquid that is drawn out of the salmon
each day, you'll make a delicious gravlax.

Tom Spag and Ham 🏠

I've been lucky to cook in Italy with Italian grandmas and I love the way they cook with a fierce passion, bossing you around the kitchen. And then insist on gallons and gallons of boiling water to cook pasta. Which means this recipe breaks the rules in a most magnifico, delizioso, molto buono way – and with not a drop of wasted water. Anna Jones inspired this recipe in her book *A Modern Way to Cook*. Cheers AJ.

MAKES: *enough for 4*
TAKES: *about 14 minutes*
FIRE: *hot embers*
KIT: *large pan, wooden spoon*

—

400g spaghetti
1.2 litres cold water
Big handful of diced ham
2 handfuls of greens (small pieces of broccoli, kale,
fresh spinach or green beans)
1 garlic clove, smashed
1 × 400g tin chopped tomatoes
Salt and pepper
Hot sauce, lemon juice, grated Parmesan, to finish

Empty the packet of spaghetti into a large pan, snapping it in half so it sits on the bottom of the pan. Add the cold water, salt and pepper and get heating over a moderate heat.
Add the diced ham, greens, garlic and chopped tomatoes. Stir occasionally, until the spaghetti is cooked. Finish with any combination of hot sauce, a squeeze of lemon, lots of grated Parmesan cheese, a twist of pepper.

Tip
— *Look for a cheap ham hock. Pick off the succulent chunks of meat and add the bone to the mix for extra flavour.*

Asian-style Foil-baked Trout

One year, on the last day of our holiday way out west, I managed to hunt down a fine Sewin, a sea trout caught from a coracle. I consulted local chef friend Scott Davis and he advised baking it whole with asian flavours. So we did and it was delicious. It fed my massive family on my birthday, we all loved it and here it is for you.

MAKES: *enough for 4*

TAKES: *25–30 minutes*

KIT: *large sheet of catering-strength foil, grill*

—

4 small or 2 large trout, gutted and slashed 3 times on each side

Fat thumb of ginger, peeled and very finely chopped

1 red chilli, deseeded and finely chopped

½ bunch of fresh coriander, finely chopped

Grated zest and juice of 1 lime

Glug of olive oil

Several splashes of soy sauce

Salt and pepper

Place the trout on the foil, bringing the sides up slightly to make a bowl – take care not to make any holes in the foil. Add the remaining ingredients to the trout and mingle them around.

Bring the foil together to make a secure parcel around the trout so it can be baked on both sides.

Carefully transfer to the grill; after 5 minutes turn it over and cook for a further 5 minutes.

Taking care not to lose any juice, open the parcel. Use your knife to check the flesh is just cooked. Warning: the smell is so savoury and delicious, you'd better all be ready to eat.

Cowboy Coffee

I've tried to live without it but can't. Maybe it's good for us?
All things in moderation, eh, and just because there isn't a
coffee shop to hand doesn't mean we should suffer. Especially
if all you need is a **pan**, a **cup** or two, some **freshly ground
coffee**, a **stick** and some **water**.

Get set up for the pan over a fire. Measure out the water you
need using the cup or cups and round it up a bit. Boil up the
water, remove from the heat and count to 3. Add 2 tablespoons
of freshly ground coffee per person / cup and leave it for
30 seconds before stirring it with a stick. Steep it for a further
2 minutes.

To encourage the grounds to sink to the bottom, flick the
surface with some cold water while tapping the sides of the
pan. Now carefully pour into the cups and add whatever you
like: sugar, cream, whisky, milk, roasted chicory root, melted
chocolate. Or just keep it short, black and strong. Wild lore
states you should pour the last one for yourself, unless there's
someone that, you know, deserves it! You fu'coffee?

Baked Fruit 🏠

Evoke the heady balmy evenings of an Indian summer with this simple recipe, where plums and peaches soften over a gentle heat and take on the smokiness of the fire, and all the sweet soft bits meld together with the crunchy chewy bits. Add a dollop of cool clotted cream and you've got yourself a pudding that is deeply satisfying.

Allow a big handful of fruit per person: apricots, peaches, plums, nectarines and cherries all work well.

Cut any large fruit in half (the smaller it is the quicker it will cook). Toss them in a roasting tray with a big knob of butter and a sprinkling of sugar. A glug of something from your hip flask can be good, try a small amount together on a spoon first to see. Place the tray over a gentle heat and allow the fruit to soften, stirring occasionally and adding water if it starts to stick. If you can, pick out the stones. After 30 minutes your delicious baked fruit will be caramelised and ready. Serve with clotted cream.

Baked Apples with an Oat Crumble

Prepare the fruit as for the recipe above, adding a handful of **raisins** and a **stick of cinnamon**. Top the lot with a crumble: mix 2 tablespoons of **brown sugar** with 1 cup of **oats**, 1 tablespoon of **flour** and a big knob of **cold butter**, and use the tips of your fingers to mix the lot together until it resembles coarse crumbs. Sprinkle over the **apples** and bake until piping hot and golden on top.

It's late, so treat yourself with a tin of custard.

Other meals you may want to consider before heading into the wild

There are two types of glass jar recipes that really lend themselves to taking outdoors. One type is the demijohn. When packed full of the ingredients needed for a butter bean casserole or ratatouille, you just take your supper from your pack, loosen the lid and sink it into a cool bed of embers to slowly cook.

Want to do better than a pot noodle? Add pre-cooked noodles to a Kilner jar along with whatever you fancy: diced tofu, green leaves, ginger, red onion, soy sauce, seaweed, sweetcorn, dried mushrooms, wedges of lime, etc. When you need to eat, pour over boiling water, give it a shake and let it all meld together for 10 minutes before eating.

Don't forget that all the usual grilled meats: lamb or pork chops, beef steaks, and grilled veg (peppers, field mushrooms, courgettes, aubergines), can be combined together as kebabs.

Afterword

At family meals we love to give thanks for our food. This coming together around a shared meal to talk about our day, to dream and bicker, holds and defines us. We go from what can so easily be an incidental act to being deliberate. Yes, the world is hard and in nature we can feel insignificant, but to come together like this is to be reminded that we are loved. When we eat in the wild, we can also show our gratitude by considering the ingredients, where they are from, the people that had a hand in them and leaving the place as it was. Enjoy.

Peace & Loaf,

Our Favourite Wild Foods

Here is a list of wild foods to forage that reads like a poem. Take care to correctly identify each one and gather when in season. Thank you to everyone who helped to compile this list via *@Tom_Herbert_* on Twitter.

— Elderflowers and Berries / Meadow Sweet

— Blackberries / Wild Strawberries / Bilberries

— Walnuts / Hazelnuts / Sweet Chestnuts

— Wild Garlic / Sorrel / Watercress / Wild Thyme / Nettles / Dandelions

— Puff Balls / St George / Truffles

— Sloes / Bullace (wild plums) / Crab Apples

— Shore Crabs / Muscles / Cockles / Razor Clams / Crayfish

— Rabbit / Venison / Horseradish / Pine Buds

— Sea Purslane / Samphire / Sea Kale / Sea Arrow Grass

How to spark a conversation

I used to have a mug with conversations starters on it that was made by my friend, Alice Hodge. It was always a good talking point and it struck me that this book could serve a similar purpose. An opportunity to open up conversations beyond the recipe. So I put a post on social media and these are a few of the responses (thank you!), plus a few of my own. And some from the mug.

Do you want a drink?

Where did you grow up?

What's your favourite smell?

Would you rather be a bird or a fish?

What have you watched lately that you enjoyed?

What in your life gives you a sense of purpose?

What are you committed to?

What are you passionate about?

What was the last thing your heart was really on fire for, and when was that?

If you could travel to any place, from any period of time, where would you go, with whom, and why?

What would your last supper be, where would you have it and with whom (dead or alive)?

What would you do if you had no fear?

What would you do if you knew you couldn't fail?

What does the future look like if things go your way?

If you could live your life again, what would you do differently from what you have done? ('Nothing' is not acceptable.)

If you won the lottery, what would you do?

If you knew you were going to die in 5 years, or 6 months, what would you do with the time?

If your life were a book, how would your story go and would it be a bestseller?

If you could write the eulogy for your funeral what would it say?

Another drink?

Are you happy?

What shall we have for breakfast?

Dough scraper

Tony, the bakery manager that scrutinised my every move as a bakery apprentice, insisted I always had a dough scraper in the back pocket of my checks. I've gone one further and always carry a stash of them to give out as my 'business card'; I wouldn't venture out without one. They are most commonly used to scrape ice from frosty car windscreens, and sometimes as giant plectrums, to swim faster (tip: swap hands occasionally or you'll do a big circle) and even once to fend off a swan. Here's how to make your own.

You will need:
— 1 page template of a dough scraper
— a plastic container (the firmer and thicker the plastic
  the better, max 2mm)
— strong scissors or secateurs
— sandpaper

Draw out the template on a flat piece of your plastic container. Cut out your dough scraper and sand off any rough edges. Ideally one of the curved sides should be filed down to a sharpish edge, useful for chopping dough and things and especially good for cleaning pans and bowls.

What will you use yours for? Post a photo with hashtags: *#mydoughscraper #WildBaking*

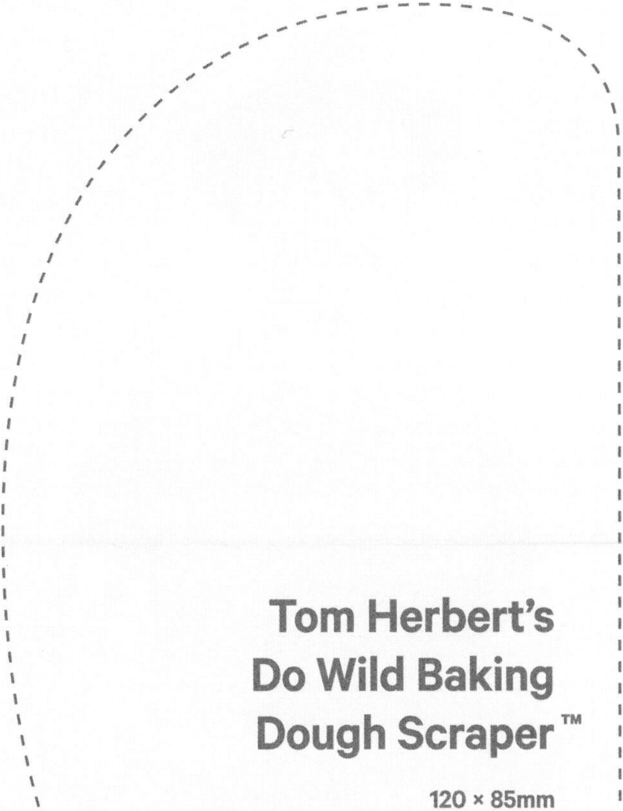

**Tom Herbert's
Do Wild Baking
Dough Scraper™**

120 × 85mm

About the Author

I've been married to Anna since we were very young; we now share our life together with four children: Milo, Beatrix, Josephine and Prudence.

I'm a fifth-generation baker on a mission to revisit the sheer awesomeness of grains when it comes to taste, nutrition and impact. If you want to assist me in any way with any of that, please let me know.

I'm co-founder of The Long Table, a community food hall supporting food hubs and local supply chains around Gloucestershire. I'm also one half of TV's Fabulous Baker Brothers. I started baking at the Hobbs House Bakery and in recent years I have baked with RCK (Refugee Community Kitchen) in Calais and Ujima Bakehouse in Kenya. In addition to baking, I also teach, write, present, mentor and I do speaking.

My dream is to one day be able to bake in space. In the meantime, perhaps we'll cross paths in some wild place with a wonderful view and possibly share a decent bottle of wine.

Find me at *thelongtableonline.com* or say hi on Instagram and Twitter *@Tom_Herbert_*

Thanks

I'd like to thank my family for always being up for it, keeping life tasty and adventurous. To my good friends, the wild and the wise, thank you so much for the many ways you fuel my fire.

Index

Italics indicate photographs

Recipes by cooking method

In a Pot

In a Tin

In the Ash

On the Embers

On a Flat Hot Stone

On a Grill

On a Stick

Books in the series

Also available

Available in print, digital and audio formats from booksellers or via our website: **thedobook.co**

To hear about events and forthcoming titles, you can find us on social media **@dobookco**, or subscribe to our newsletter

Conversion Chart

Measurements

Cup conversions
1 cup filled to the top or the fill line will yield:
— 280g sourdough starter
— 240g/ml water (or other liquid)
— 200g grain / sugar / dried fruit
— 120g flour (equals two hands cupped together)
— 110g oats

Weigh or measure 240g/ml water using digital scales at home, pour into your chosen measuring cup and mark off the fill line on the cup (ideally it would be full to the brim).

Other useful volume measurements
1 glug oil = 1 tablespoon / 15 ml
Pinch of salt = 5g
Good pinch of salt = 6g
Big pinch of salt = 8g

Temperature

Flippin' HOT
240–350°C / 460–660°F

HOT
200–240°C / 390–460°F

HOT-ish
160–200°C / 320–390°F